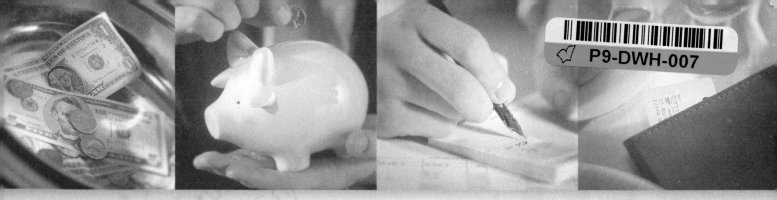

MANAGING OUR FINANCES

GOD'S WAY

A portion of this *Managing Our Finances God's Way* is based on the
Biblical Financial Study, © 1986, 2003 Crown Financial™ Ministries, Inc.,
the Biblical Financial Study Practical Application Workbook, © 1997, 2003 Crown Financial™
Ministries, Inc., and Free and Clear, © 2005 Crown Financial™ Ministries, Inc. For more
information on Crown Financial™ Ministries contact www.crown.org.

PurposeDriven®

Published by Purpose Driven® Publishing.
20 Empire
Lake Forest, CA 92630
www.purposedriven.com

Scripture quotations noted AMP are from the AMPLIFIED® BIBLE, © 1954, 1958, 1962, 1964,
1965, 1987 by The Lockman Foundation. Used by permission. (www.Lockman.org)

Scripture quotations noted CEV are from THE CONTEMPORARY ENGLISH VERSION
(American Bible Society, 1865 Broadway, New York, NY 10023)
and are used by permission.

Scripture quotations noted GWT are from GOD'S WORD TRANSLATION. God's Word
Translation is a copyrighted work of God's Word to the Nations Bible Society. Quotations are
used by permission. Copyright 1995 by God's Word to the Nations Bible Society.
All rights reserved.

Scripture quotations noted KJV are from THE KING JAMES VERSION.

Scripture quotations noted LB are from THE LIVING BIBLE (copyright 1971 by Tyndale House
Publishers, Wheaton, Illinois) and are used by permission.

Scripture quotations noted MSG are from THE MESSAGE by Eugene H. Peterson. Copyright
1993, 1994, 1995, 1996, and 2000. Used by permission of NavPress Publishing Group.
All rights reserved.

Scripture quotations noted NASB are from the NEW AMERICAN STANDARD BIBLE, © 1960,
1962, 1963, 1968, 1971, 1972, 1973, 1975, 1977 by The Lockman Foundation.
Used by permission.

Scripture quotations noted NIV are from the HOLY BIBLE, NEW INTERNATIONAL VERSION.
Copyright 1973, 1978, and 1984 by International Bible Society. Used by permission of
Zondervan Bible Publishing House. All rights reserved.

Scripture quotations marked NKJV are taken from the NEW KING JAMES VERSION. Copyright
© 1979, 1980, 1982 by Thomas Nelson, Inc. Used by permission.
All rights reserved.

Scripture quotations noted NLT are from THE HOLY BIBLE, NEW LIVING TRANSLATION.
Copyright 1996. Used by permission of Tyndale House Publishers, Inc.,
Wheaton, IL 60189. All rights reserved.

Scripture quotations noted TEV are from TODAY'S ENGLISH VERSION (American Bible
Society, 1865 Broadway, New York, NY 10023) and are used by permission.

TABLE OF CONTENTS

Welcome to *Managing Our Finances God's Way*. Over the next seven weeks, expect to be convinced that God deeply cares about your finances.

Many of us think we don't need help with our finances. We're adults, after all, and we can make our own decisions. But the truth is, we all need help—and that's why this study has been created.

There are many experts out there who offer advice, but not everyone can get to know an expert. God has given you this group to be your "experts." As you work through these seven lessons, you'll be surprised to discover how much your group already knows.

Over the next few weeks, you will confront topics you may not always enjoy or feel comfortable with. I encourage you to persevere. God never said life would be easy, but he did promise to reward the diligent.

One step we'll be encouraging you to take in the coming weeks is to find a spiritual partner. Ideally, this is someone in your group you can check in with at least once a week through a phone call, e-mail, or a chat over coffee. Spiritual partners monitor each others progress, help sort out questions, and pray for each other as they grow together in godly understanding. This type of back-up system is completely biblical and life changing!

Along with the group study lessons, you'll find easy-to-use tools to guide you through this program. These tools are included in each lesson and there are additional copies in the back of your workbook. We have also included a Resource CD in the back of your workbook that contains electronic versions of these worksheets. The best part about the electronic files is that they do the calculations for you automatically. You will also find contact information to help answer your questions, and suggestions for how to keep your financial plans on track, making them lifelong habits.

Let me take a minute to explain the features of this study.

- *Catching Up:* You will open each meeting with an opportunity for everyone to check in with each other about how you are doing with the weekly assignments. Accountability is a key to success in this study!

- *Key Verse:* Each week you will find a key verse or Scripture passage for your group to read together. If someone in the group has a different translation, ask them to read it aloud so the group can get a bigger picture of the meaning of the passage.

- *Video Lesson:* There is a twenty minute video lesson for the group to watch together each week. Follow along by filling in the lesson outlines in the workbook.

- *Discussion Questions:* Each video segment is complemented by several questions for group discussion. Please don't feel like you have to answer every single question. The material in this study is meant to be your servant, not your master, so there is no reason to rush through your answers. Give everyone ample opportunity to share their thoughts. If you don't get through all of the discussion questions, that's okay.

- *Living on Purpose:* In his book, *The Purpose Driven® Life*, Rick Warren identifies God's five purposes for our lives. They are worship, fellowship, discipleship, ministry, and evangelism. We will focus on one of these five purposes in each lesson, and discuss how it relates to the subject of the study. This section is very important, so please be sure to leave time for it.

- *Prayer Direction:* At the end of each session we give you suggestions about how to pray together. Please don't skip this very important time with your group. Good intentions are one thing; but the power of prayer is indispensable. Praying together is one of the greatest privileges of small group life. Don't take it for granted.

- *Putting It into Practice:* This is where the rubber meets the road. We don't want to be just hearers of the Word. We also need to be doers of the Word (James 1:22). This section of the study explains the assignments we would like you to complete before your next meeting. These assignments are application exercises that will help you put into practice the truths you have discussed in the lesson. **We will not ask you to share your financial information with each other**, but we will ask you to keep each other accountable to do the work and follow through with your commitments.

The bottom line of this study is that you will get out of it what you are willing to put into it. You can't reap a harvest if you don't sow the seeds. In the same way, you can't expect to reap a harvest of knowledge and new habits from this study if you're not willing to roll up your sleeves and do the work. As the Bible says, *"Let us not become weary in doing good, for at the proper time we will reap a harvest if we do not give up"* (Galatians 6:9 NIV).

Some of these exercises may open your eyes to painful truths about your current financial situation. But please don't let fear or discouragement keep you from the truth. The Bible tells us that freedom begins with knowing the truth (John 8:32). So we have to take an honest look at where we are in order to determine how to get where we want to be. If you want to be financially free, you might have to make some tough choices and discipline yourself to make changes in your values and lifestyle. The Bible says, *"No discipline seems pleasant at the time, but painful. Later on, however, it produces a harvest of righteousness and peace for those who have been trained by it"* (Hebrews 12:11 NIV). If you want to experience the peace of God in your finances, then you have to follow God's plan for your finances. But be encouraged—God wants you to be financially free, and *"nothing is impossible with God"* (Luke 1:37 NIV)!

I'm so glad you're here! May God richly bless you as you discover his principles and become, at long last, financially free.

Chris Goulard
Pastor of Stewardship, Saddleback Church

How to Use this Video Curriculum

Follow these simple steps for a successful small group meeting:

1. Open your group meeting by using the *Looking Ahead/Catching Up* section of your study guide.

2. Watch the video lesson together and follow along in the outlines in this study guide. Each video lesson is about 20 minutes long.

3. Complete the rest of the discussion materials for each session, including the *Living on Purpose* section.

4. Review the *Putting It into Practice* assignments and commit to doing them before your next meeting.

It's just that simple. Have a great study together!

> These assignments are application exercises that will help you put into practice the truths you have discussed in the lesson. **We will not ask you to share your financial information with each other,** but we will ask you to keep each other accountable to do the work and follow through with your commitments.

INTRODUCTION

THE BIG PICTURE

RICK WARREN

INTRODUCTION: THE BIG PICTURE

LOOKING AHEAD . . . . 10 MINUTES

- Welcome any new members to your small group. Read and discuss the *Purpose Driven Group Guidelines* on page 104 of this study guide.

- What do you hope to get out of this study?

- Opening Prayer: Pray that God will help you to be open to what he wants to teach you through this series.

KEY VERSE . . . . 2 MINUTES

> **HOST TIPS:** Ask someone to read the verse below aloud. If anyone has a different translation, ask him or her to read this as well to expand your understanding.

Tell them to use their money to do good . . .
By doing this they will be storing up real treasure for
themselves in heaven—it is the only safe
investment for eternity!

1 Timothy 6:18a, 19a (LB)

 Watch the video lesson now and follow along in your outline. . . . . **25** MINUTES

Everything you have is a gift from God.

God wants you to partner with him in accomplishing his purposes on earth . . . God really isn't interested in watching you fulfill *your* dream for your life; he wants you to fulfill *his* dream for your life—the reason he put you on this planet.

If Christ is truly your king, then you live in a kingdom different from the kingdoms of the world. Christ's kingdom has a different set of rules, a different set of values, and a different economy.

- In Christ's kingdom, we understand the purpose for earthly wealth is to invest it

  in _____ .

   > *[19]"Do not store up for yourselves treasures on earth, where moth and rust destroy, and where thieves break in and steal. [20]But store up for yourselves treasures in heaven, where moth and rust do not destroy, and where thieves do not break in and steal." (Matthew 6:19–20 NIV)*

God's five purposes for our lives:

We are all called to:

- Worship

- Fellowship

- Grow like Christ

- Serve others

- Be on-mission for God in the world

   > *"I will bless those who bless you, and whoever curses you I will curse; and all peoples on earth will be blessed through you."*
   > *(Genesis 12:3 NIV)*

God desires to work through ordinary _____ with ordinary _____ .

   > *Do not conform any longer to the pattern of this world, but be transformed by the renewing of your mind. (Romans 12:2a NIV)*

The World's Pattern

God's Pattern

The Big Picture

God wants to do something of eternal _____ through your life.

> *Where there is no vision, the people are unrestrained . . .*
> (Proverbs 29:18a NASB)

God's vision changes how we live, in every way:

- Our values

- Our priorities

- Our way of life

56% of all divorces are the result of financial pressure.

— Gallup Poll

God wants you to be financially free because he has a plan and a purpose for your life. But if you're tied up in financial bondage, you can't be free to be used the way God wants to use you.

BIBLE FACTS

- There are 2,350 verses in the Bible about money. (All of these verses are referenced on the Resource CD.)

- One out of every six verses in Matthew, Mark, and Luke is about material possessions.

- Nearly half of Jesus' parables are about possessions.

- Jesus spoke more about money and how to use it than he did about heaven and hell combined.

Two primary misconceptions about money:

First misconception: Money is _____ .

> *"The love of money is the root of all evil . . ."* (1 Timothy 6:10a KJV)

If you make money your god, it's going to plague you like the devil.

Second misconception: Money is the _____ .

> *¹⁰Those who love money will never have enough. How absurd to think that wealth brings true happiness! ¹¹ᵃThe more you have, the more people come to help you spend it . . .* (Ecclesiastes 5:10–11a NLT)

> *". . . a man's life does not consist in the abundance of his possessions."* (Luke 12:15b NIV)

> *"What shall it profit a man, if he shall gain the whole world, and lose his own soul?"* (Mark 8:36 KJV)

- **Financial freedom is not determined by how much money you make. It's determined by _____ .**

> *. . . stupid people spend their money as fast as they get it.* (Proverbs 21:20b TEV)

- **In other words, most of us don't have a _____ problem. We have a _____ problem.**

> *²²But the fruit of the Spirit is love, joy, peace, patience, kindness, goodness, faithfulness, ²³gentleness and self-control. Against such things there is no law.* (Galatians 5:22–23 NIV)

- **Without self-control, our** _____ **capacity will always exceed our** _____ **capacity.**

One day we are all going to stand before God, and he is going to ask each of us two questions:

- What did you do with my son, Jesus Christ?

- What did you do with what I gave you?

"If you are untrustworthy about worldly wealth, who will trust you with the true riches of heaven?" (Luke 16:11 NLT)

[18a]Tell them to use their money to do good . . . [19a]by doing this they will be storing up real treasure for themselves in heaven—it is the only safe investment for eternity! (1 Timothy 6:18a, 19a LB)

The Prayer of Agur

Don't let me be too poor or too rich.
Give me just what I need. If I have too much to eat,
I might forget about you; if I don't have enough,
I might steal and disgrace your name.

Proverbs 30:8–9 (CEV)

Godliness with contentment is great gain. (1 Timothy 6:6 NIV)

A new definition of what it means to be wealthy:

A truly wealthy person is a person who is _____ with what he or she has.

INTRODUCTION: THE BIG PICTURE

DISCUSSION QUESTIONS . . . . 40 MINUTES

1. Did you know before this lesson that God has given us so many biblical principles for our finances? How does this knowledge affect your attitude toward God?

2. Look back at the wheel diagram in the lesson. Does God's pattern make sense to you? Does it surprise you that the world's way and God's way are exactly opposite? Discuss those differences and how God's way is in your best interest.

3. How content are you with your present financial situation? Contentment does not mean having everything you want. It means being satisfied with—and grateful for—what you have.

4. What difference does it make when you consider that your money is on loan from God? Where will your money go, and how will it be used, once you have passed into eternity?

5. Rick reminded us that God wants us to love people and use money, not the other way around. When we use our money for God, what is the potential outcome?

6. What does financial freedom look like from God's perspective? How would you live if you were financially free?

LIVING ON PURPOSE . . . . 10 MINUTES

Ministry

In the video, Rick talks about God's five purposes for your life, one of which is ministry. Think of an area of service God may be pointing you towards that lines up with your life purpose. We realize this is a huge subject. Try to get started on it while you're together in this session. Be prepared to further discuss your answers with your group at your next meeting.

PRAYER DIRECTION . . . . 10 MINUTES

As you close your meeting, each of you take turns praying brief prayers of thanksgiving for what God has given you. After everyone has finished their prayers of gratitude, then pray for each other's prayer requests.

PUTTING IT INTO PRACTICE

Complete these assignments before your next meeting.

1. Review the verses in this lesson and ask God to give you his perspective on money. If you have time, look up some of the other references to money and possessions. Whatever your attitude has been up until now, whatever your current financial situation, God wants to work through you for his eternal purposes. The only thing stopping him is you. If you truly want financial freedom, God's way is the only way.

2. One of the most important ways to get control of our finances is to learn where our money is going. It is also the first step toward putting together a spending plan, which we will be doing in the coming weeks. Starting now, we are all going to write down every financial transaction we make—every purchase made, every bill paid, every dollar spent. Because holding on to receipts can become cumbersome, some people find it helpful to carry a small pad in a purse or car so it will always be handy for recording these transactions. On page 13, there is a *Transaction Record* that you can use as well. Whatever your system is, you need to know three things about every purchase you make: the date, the exact amount, and what you purchased. Do this faithfully until the next meeting, and then we will check in as a group to see how we did.

3. In his book, *The Purpose Driven® Life,* Rick Warren presents the concept of SHAPE: **S**piritual gifts, **H**eart (passions and interests), **A**bilities, **P**ersonality, **E**xperiences. Rick also said in today's lesson, "God wants to do something of eternal significance through your life." As you consider that statement in light of your God-given SHAPE, what do you think God's vision might be for your life? What do you think he would do through you if you were living in financial freedom? Turn to page 14 where you will find space to capture your thoughts and ideas throughout the week.

WORKBOOK EXPLANATION

Each week there will be a financial assignment to complete as part of the study. This workbook contains an explanation of the assignments, a completed sample to assist you, and a blank worksheet for you to fill out. We suggest you use pencil so you can easily make changes. If you are married, please complete the forms with your spouse.

Though we will not ask you to show this information to the group, we will ask you to discuss how the assignment went each week. It is important to you, and to the group as a whole, that you faithfully complete this work.

There are also additional copies of the forms in the back of the workbook, perforated so you can easily remove them and make photocopies. Students of this study are authorized to make photocopies of the forms for their personal use, but for no other purpose.

The CD-ROM located in the back of this workbook contains many helpful items. All the forms in the workbook are also in electronic form on the disc, along with a debt repayment calculator, screen saver, money scriptures (2,350 verses about finances), and much more. The benefit of using the electronic worksheets is that the calculations will be done automatically for you.

Transaction Record

One of the most important ways to get control of our finances is to learn where our money is going. It is also the first step toward putting together a *Spending Plan*, which we will be doing in the coming weeks. Starting now, record your income and spending for 30 days. This will help you more accurately determine what you are actually earning and where it is going.

Write down every financial transaction you make—every check deposited, every purchase made, every bill paid, every dollar spent. Because holding on to receipts can become cumbersome, some people find it helpful to carry a small pad in a purse or car so it will always be handy for recording these transactions, while others may choose to record them in their PDA. On page 13, and in the back of your workbook, there is a *Transaction Record* that you can use as well. The Resource CD has a similar form, *Spending Register*, that you can also print out to record your transactions. Whatever your system is, you need to know three things about every purchase you make: (1) the date; (2) the exact amount; and, (3) what you purchased.

If you would like to work ahead, you can begin adding these transactions into the *Monthly Expenses* worksheet on page 72. This will be an assignment for a future lesson.

TRANSACTION RECORD

(If you desire to have a transaction/check register for your spending categories, please use this worksheet.)

Date	Check #	Transaction	Spending Category	Deposit	Withdrawal
1/2/06	receipt	Dinner with Bob and Carol	Entertainment	$	$ 54.29
1/6/06	1001	Discovery Card	Debt Repayment	$	$ 25.00
1/6/06	Cash	Gum	Groceries	$	$ 1.95
1/6/06	ATM	Cash	Cash	$	$ 100.00
1/10/06	ATM	Roy's (included $20.00 cash)	Groceries	$	$ 85.29
1/11/06	1002	Jefferson Mutual	Mortgage	$	$ 1,200.89
1/11/06	1003	Dusty Canyon Homeowners Association	Housing	$	$ 200.00
1/15/06	DEP	Cell Phone Reimbursement	Utilities	$ 100.00	$
				$	$
				$	$
				$	$
				$	$
				$	$
				$	$
				$	$
				$	$
				$	$
				$	$
				$	$
				$	$
				$	$
				$	$
				$	$
				$	$
				$	$
				$	$
				$	$
				$	$
				$	$
				$	$
				$	$
				$	$
				$	$
				$	$
				$	$
				$	$
				$	$
				$	$
				$	$
				$	$
				$	$
				$	$
				$	$

PurposeDriven®

TRANSACTION RECORD

CROWN FINANCIAL MINISTRIES

(If you desire to have a transaction/check register for your spending categories, please use this worksheet.)

Date	Check #	Transaction	Spending Category	Deposit	Withdrawal
				$	$
				$	$
				$	$
				$	$
				$	$
				$	$
				$	$
				$	$
				$	$
				$	$
				$	$
				$	$
				$	$
				$	$
				$	$
				$	$
				$	$
				$	$
				$	$
				$	$
				$	$
				$	$
				$	$
				$	$
				$	$
				$	$
				$	$
				$	$
				$	$
				$	$
				$	$
				$	$
				$	$
				$	$
				$	$
				$	$
				$	$
				$	$
				$	$
				$	$
				$	$
				$	$
				$	$
				$	$
				$	$
				$	$
				$	$
				$	$
				$	$

WHAT IS GOD'S VISION FOR MY LIFE?

SESSION ONE

DEDICATE IT ALL TO GOD

CHIP INGRAM

CATCHING UP .... 10 MINUTES

- Opening Prayer

- Are you beginning to see God's role in your finances in a different light? Were you successful in tracking your spending this past week? If this has been a struggle for you, don't give up! Persistence is the key to any healthy habit.

- Two or three of you briefly share what you discovered as you journaled about your life purpose. (Consider making this a group discussion topic down the road, or even using *40 Days of Purpose* as your next group study.)

KEY VERSE .... 2 MINUTES

> **HOST TIPS:** Ask someone to read the verse below aloud. If anyone has a different translation, ask him or her to read this as well to expand your understanding.

*Everything in the heavens and on earth is yours,
O LORD, and this is your kingdom. We adore you as the
one who is over all things. Riches and honor come
from you alone, for you rule over everything.
Power and might are in your hand, and it is at your
discretion that people are made great
and given strength.*

1 Chronicles 29:11b–12 (NLT)

 Watch the video lesson now and follow along in your outline. . . . . **25** MINUTES

God _____ everything.

You are his _____ .

> *The earth is the LORD's, and everything in it, the world, and all who live in it.* (Psalm 24:1 NIV)

> *"The silver is mine and the gold is mine," declares the LORD Almighty.* (Haggai 2:8 NIV)

> *But remember the LORD your God, for it is he who gives you the ability to produce wealth . . .* (Deuteronomy 8:18a NIV)

> [19b]*You are not your own;* [20a]*you were bought at a price.* (1 Corinthians 6:19b–20a NIV)

THE "OIKONOMIA PRINCIPLE"

All that we are and all that we have belongs to God. He has temporarily entrusted it to us to manage according to his wishes.

Stewardship of God's property is not just about money. We are stewards of all these gifts as well:

• _____

> *Teach us to make the most of our time, so that we may grow in wisdom.* (Psalm 90:12 NLT)

• _____

> *. . . a prudent wife is from the LORD.* (Proverbs 19:14b NIV)

- _____

    Children are a gift from the LORD; they are a reward from him.
    (Psalm 127:3 NLT)

- _____

    *[11]"And if you are untrustworthy about worldly wealth, who will trust
    you with the true riches of heaven? [12]And if you are not faithful with
    other people's money, why should you be trusted with money of your
    own?"* (Luke 16:11–12 NLT)

- _____

    *God has given gifts to each of you from his great variety of spiritual
    gifts. Manage them well so that God's generosity can flow through you.*
    (1 Peter 4:10 NLT)

- _____

    *[1]People should think of us as servants of Christ and managers who are
    entrusted with God's mysteries. [2]Managers are required to be
    trustworthy.* (1 Corinthians 4:1–2 GWT)

- _____

    For the overseer must be above reproach as God's steward . . .
    (Titus 1:7a NASB)

Every good thing bestowed and every perfect gift is from above, coming down from the Father of lights, with whom there is no variation, or shifting shadow. (James 1:17 NASB)

¹Let a man regard us in this manner, as servants of Christ, and stewards of the mysteries of God. ²In this case, moreover, it is required of stewards that one be found trustworthy. (1 Corinthians 4:1–2 NASB)

Five reasons to dedicate it all to God:

1. **It all belongs to _____ .**

2. **You are his _____ .**

3. **You cannot serve _____ .**

4. **You can make an impact on _____ .**

5. **God blesses that which we _____ to him.**

This is the wisest financial decision you will ever make—to do finances in a way that honors Christ. Make the decision to give your all to him.

DISCUSSION QUESTIONS . . . . 40 MINUTES

1. The dynamic of Chip's relationship with John is exactly the dynamic that God wants in his relationship with you.

   a. Chip started asking: "What would John want me to do?"

   b. Chip became more faithful in handling John's money than his own.

   c. Chip and John became best friends.

   What parallels can you draw from this story to your personal relationship with God and your attitude toward your finances? How are they related?

2. How would your financial habits be likely to change if you asked every day, "How does God want me to spend his money?" Think about Chip's example of putting the checkbook near his watch and keys. What will you do to remind yourself from time to time that you are a steward of God's resources?

3. Think about the people you may meet in heaven one day who were helped by your stewardship of God's resources. How does this make you feel about what you are learning in this study?

4. Review the "Oikonomia Principle." How does recognizing God's ultimate ownership of all things alter your life view?

LIVING ON PURPOSE . . . . 10 MINUTES

Evangelism

Think about how Chip was able to touch people's lives for Christ through his relationship with John Saville. God wants you to know that how you use your financial resources is critical to fulfilling the purpose of evangelism in your life. Look for an opportunity to meet someone's needs this week as a way of sharing Christ's love. In the next session, be ready to tell your group about your experience.

PRAYER DIRECTION . . . . 10 MINUTES

Ask God to open your eyes to the opportunities he brings your way to share the love of Christ with others. Ask him to give you his heart for people.

Ask God to help you loosen your grip on what he has given you so that his generosity can flow through you.

PUTTING IT INTO PRACTICE

Complete these assignments before your next meeting.

1. This week we will be filling out a *Personal Financial Profile*, which looks at "What I Own" and "What I Owe." There are worksheets and instructions on pages 22–24, or you can use the Resource CD that came with this study. Because this information is personal, we will not be sharing it with each other in the group. We will, however, check in with each other next week to see how we did with the exercise.

2. Ask God to prepare you for relinquishing control of all you have to him. On page 27, you'll find a form called *Quit Claim Deed*. Its purpose is to serve as a tangible reminder of this partnership you're about to enter into with God. Prior to your next meeting, complete the deed, but do not sign it yet. Be sure to bring the deed with you next time, as you'll be signing and witnessing these documents together as a group.

3. Be sure you continue to track your expenses over the next week!

PERSONAL FINANCIAL PROFILE

This worksheet is designed to give you a current picture of your financial situation. Accountants would refer to this page as a "balance sheet." For the purposes of this study, it is not necessary to be precise to the penny; rather, give your best estimate of the current value of each asset ("What I Own"). When you have entered each asset, add up the total and enter it in the "Total Assets" box.

For the liabilities ("What I Owe"), look at your most recent statement for each debt to find the most accurate figures. Record all of your debts, and then enter the subtotals in the appropriate boxes. To calculate your Net Worth, subtract your Total Debt from your Total Assets. Don't be discouraged if you owe more than you own. That's not uncommon. The purpose for this study is to help you improve your financial picture. But you have to start with an honest assessment of your current position in order to know what steps you need to take. We recommend that you complete this form once each year to gauge your financial progress.

Remember, these worksheets are available on the Resource CD, where the calculations will be done automatically for you.

》PurposeDriven®

PERSONAL FINANCIAL PROFILE

CROWN FINANCIAL MINISTRIES

Name: John and Jane Sample

Date: January 1

WHAT I OWN (Assets)
(Please fill in all sections as well as you can)

CATEGORY	CURRENT VALUES	
Checking Accounts	$	2,061.23
Savings Accounts	$	568.00
Money Market Accounts	$	1,827.00
Certificates of Deposit	$	-
Stocks / Bonds / Mutual Funds	$	-
Life Insurance (Cash Value)	$	-
Primary Residence (Market Value)	$	250,000.00
Other Real Estate	$	-
Car #1 Resale Value	$	6,000.00
Car #2 Resale Value	$	2,400.00
Car #3 Resale Value	$	-
Other Personal Property	$	2,500.00
IRAs / Retirement Funds / 401K	$	10,000.00
Other (i.e., Business . . .)	$	-
TOTAL ASSETS:	$	**275,356.23**

WHAT I OWE (Liabilities)
(Please fill in all sections as well as you can)

CATEGORY	DEBT NAME	MONTHLY PAYMENT	INTEREST %	TOTAL BALANCE
Mortgage / Rent	House Payment	$ 1,200.89	6.00 %	$ 198,224.00
Additional Real Estate Loan		$ -	%	$ -
Car #1 Payment	Toyota Camry	$ 198.00	5.50 %	$ 3,500.00
Car #2 Payment		$ -	%	$ -
Car #3 Payment		$ -	%	$ -
		$	%	$
		$	%	$
Mortgage and Car Debt Subtotal:		$ 1,398.89		$ 201,724.00
Credit Cards	VISA	$ 100.00	18.00 %	$ 2,500.00
	MC	$ 120.00	15.00 %	$ 5,725.00
		$ -	%	$ -
		$ -	%	$ -
		$ -	%	$ -
		$ -	%	$ -
		$ -	%	$ -
		$ -	%	$ -
Other Debts (personal loans, student loans, business debt, medical, legal, IRS, etc.)		$	%	$
	Student Loan	$ 124.36	4.50 %	$ 12,150.00
		$	%	$
		$	%	$
		$	%	$
		$	%	$
Credit Cards and Other Subtotals:		$ 344.36		$ 20,375.00
	TOTAL MONTHLY PAYMENTS:	$ 1,743.25	**TOTAL DEBT:**	$ 222,099.00
	TOTAL ASSETS – TOTAL DEBT =		**NET WORTH:**	$ 53,257.23

))) PurposeDriven®

PERSONAL FINANCIAL PROFILE

CROWN FINANCIAL MINISTRIES

Name:

Date:

WHAT I OWN (Assets)
(Please fill in all sections as well as you can)

CATEGORY	CURRENT VALUES	
Checking Accounts	$	
Savings Accounts	$	
Money Market Accounts	$	
Certificates of Deposit	$	
Stocks / Bonds / Mutual Funds	$	
Life Insurance (Cash Value)	$	
Primary Residence (Market Value)	$	
Other Real Estate	$	
Car #1 Resale Value	$	
Car #2 Resale Value	$	
Car #3 Resale Value	$	
Other Personal Property	$	
IRAs / Retirement Funds / 401K	$	
Other (i.e., Business . . .)	$	
	TOTAL ASSETS:	$

WHAT I OWE (Liabilities)
(Please fill in all sections as well as you can)

CATEGORY	DEBT NAME	MONTHLY PAYMENT	INTEREST %	TOTAL BALANCE
Mortgage / Rent		$	%	$
Additional Real Estate Loan		$	%	$
Car #1 Payment		$	%	$
Car #2 Payment		$	%	$
Car #3 Payment		$	%	$
		$	%	$
		$	%	$
Mortgage and Car Debt Subtotal:		$		$
Credit Cards		$	%	$
		$	%	$
		$	%	$
		$	%	$
		$	%	$
		$	%	$
		$	%	$
		$	%	$
Other Debts (personal loans, student loans, business debt, medical, legal, IRS, etc.)		$	%	$
		$	%	$
		$	%	$
		$	%	$
		$	%	$
		$	%	$
Credit Cards and Other Subtotals:		$		$
	TOTAL MONTHLY PAYMENTS:	$	**TOTAL DEBT:**	$
	TOTAL ASSETS – TOTAL DEBT =		**NET WORTH:**	$

THE QUIT CLAIM DEED

This exercise symbolizes a transfer of the ownership of our possessions to the Lord. This deed is not a legally binding document; it is only for your use. The *Quit Claim Deed* exercise is a two step process:

- **Step One:** Fill in your name at the top of the deed. Do not fill in the date yet. Then, in the middle of the deed, prayerfully write a list of your possessions for which you are willing to acknowledge God's ultimate ownership.

- **Step Two:** At your next group meeting, sign the *Quit Claim Deed* (page 27 or 119) at the bottom, fill in the date at the top, and ask others in your group to witness your signature. In this way, you are agreeing to hold one another accountable in recognizing God as owner of your possessions.

In addition, you will find a small "Quit Claim Card" on the *Key Verses* page (page 111) in the back of this study guide. This card is to remind you of your completed *Quit Claim Deed*. We recommend that you date this card and tape it inside the cover of your Bible as a permanent reminder of your acknowledgement that God owns everything.

Quit Claim Deed

This Quit Claim Deed, Made the <u>15th</u> day of <u>February</u>

From: <u>John and Jane Sample</u>

To: The Lord

I (we) hereby transfer to the Lord the ownership of the following possessions:

Home	Golf clubs
John's car	Sewing machine
Jane's car	Stamp collection
Clothes	John's job
Savings account	Wedding rings
Boat	Children's educational fund
Furniture	Antique piano
Rental property	IBM stock
Retirement account	Pension fund
TV	

Stewards of the possessions above:

<u>John Sample</u>

<u>Jane Sample</u>

Witnesses who hold me (us) accountable in the recognition of the Lord's ownership:

_____

_____

_____

_____

This instrument is not a binding legal document and cannot be used to transfer property.

Quit Claim Deed

This Quit Claim Deed, Made the _____ day of _____

From: _____

To: The Lord

I (we) hereby transfer to the Lord the ownership of the following possessions:

_____

_____

_____

_____

_____

_____

_____

_____

_____

_____

Stewards of the possessions above:

_____

_____

Witnesses who hold me (us) accountable
in the recognition of the Lord's ownership:

_____

_____

_____

_____

This instrument is not a binding legal document and cannot be used to transfer property.

NOTES

SESSION TWO

2

PLAN YOUR SPENDING
RON BLUE

CATCHING UP . . . . 10 MINUTES

- Opening prayer.

- Please pull out the *Quit Claim Deed* you completed in preparation for today. First, sign your own deed (both spouses, if married), and then pass it to someone else in the group so they can witness it for you. As you do this, one or two of you share what it felt like to fill out the *Quit Claim Deed* and dedicate your possessions to the Lord. Also, fill out the "Quit Claim Card" on page 111 and tape it in the front cover of your Bible as a reminder of this event.

- Did you complete your *Personal Financial Profile?*

- Were you able to share the love of Christ with someone by helping to meet their needs? If so, tell the group about your experience.

KEY VERSE . . . . 2 MINUTES

> **HOST TIPS:** Ask someone to read aloud the following verse. If anyone has a different translation, ask him or her to read it to expand your understanding of the passage.

Good planning and hard work lead to prosperity,
but hasty shortcuts lead to poverty.

Proverbs 21:5 (NLT)

PLAN YOUR SPENDING

 Watch the video lesson now and follow along in your outline. **· 20** MINUTES

FINANCIAL PLANNING

Allocating limited financial resources to unlimited spending alternatives.

FRAMEWORK FOR OUR FINANCES: PRINCIPLES, PRIORITIES, PLANNING

Four Biblical Principles of Money Management

1. **Spend less than you** _____ .

    Dishonest money dwindles away, but he who gathers money little by little makes it grow. (Proverbs 13:11 NIV)

    The wise man saves for the future, but the foolish man spends whatever he gets. (Proverbs 21:20 LB)

2. **Avoid the use of** _____ .

    The rich rule over the poor, and the borrower is servant to the lender. (Proverbs 22:7 NIV)

3. **Build an** _____ **fund.**

    ⁶Go to the ant, you sluggard! Consider her ways and be wise, ⁷which, having no captain, overseer or ruler, ⁸provides her supplies in the summer, and gathers her food in the harvest. (Proverbs 6:6–8 NKJV)

4. **Set** _____ **goals.**

    I press on toward the goal for the prize of the upward call of God in Christ Jesus. (Philippians 3:14 NASB)

MANAGING OUR FINANCES

Setting Priorities

The World's Priorities	God's Priorities	
1. Lifestyle	1. Giving	} Productive
2. Taxes	2. Saving and Investing	
3. Debt Repayment	3. Debt Repayment	} Obligations
4. Saving and Investing	4. Taxes	
5. Giving	5. Lifestyle	
Result: Overspending	**Result:** Contentment	

God's Priorities

1. **Giving**

   Remember this: Whoever sows sparingly will also reap sparingly, and whoever sows generously will also reap generously. (2 Corinthians 9:6 NIV)

   On the first day of every week, each one of you should set aside a sum of money in keeping with his income, saving it up, so that when I come no collections will have to be made. (1 Corinthians 16:2 NIV)

   Giving is a _____ .

2. **Saving and Investing**

   A _____ bit over a _____ time frame makes

   a _____ difference.

3. **Debt Repayment**

   The wicked borrow and do not repay, but the righteous give generously. (Psalm 37:21 NIV)

   If I borrow money, I am _____ to repay it.

4. **Taxes**

   Give everyone what you owe him: If you owe taxes, pay taxes . . . (Romans 13:7a NIV)

   . . . "Give to Caesar what is Caesar's, and to God what is God's." (Matthew 22:21b NIV)

5. Lifestyle

a. _____ for my family.

If anyone does not provide for his relatives, and especially for his immediate family, he has denied the faith and is worse than an unbeliever. (1 Timothy 5:8 NIV)

b. Have a lifestyle I am _____ with.

⁶But godliness with contentment is great gain. ⁷For we brought nothing into the world, and we can take nothing out of it. ⁸But if we have food and clothing, we will be content with that. (1 Timothy 6:6–8 NIV)

c. _____ what God has given me.

Command those who are rich in this present world not to be arrogant nor to put their hope in wealth, which is so uncertain, but to put their hope in God, who richly provides us with everything for our enjoyment. (1 Timothy 6:17 NIV)

Planning

• There is no such thing as an _____ financial decision.

• The longer the perspective, the better the financial _____ .

• Financial _____ : Giving up today's desires for future benefits.

Five Final Instructions:

1. Pray together for God's _____ .

2. Look _____ at where you are.

3. _____ your needs and goals.

4. Prepare a _____ plan.

5. Practice keeping good _____ .

DISCUSSION QUESTIONS . . . . 40 MINUTES

1. Review and discuss the "Four Biblical Principles of Money Management":

Four Biblical Principles of Money Management

1) Spend less than you earn.
2) Avoid the use of debt.
3) Build an emergency fund.
4) Set long-term goals.

Which of these principles presents the greatest challenge for you? Why?

2. What is the first step you can take toward overcoming that challenge? Are you willing to commit to the group that you will take that step before your next meeting? Examples:

- **Spend less:** go to fewer movies; eat out less often; make your own coffee, etc.

- **Avoid debt:** cut up a credit card; throw away all the credit card offers you get in the mail; don't spend money that is not in your checking account, etc.

- **Build an emergency fund:** decide an amount to set aside each week; open a savings account; set up an automatic deposit into the account, etc.

- **Set long-term goals:** get out of debt; save for college; buy a house, etc.

3. Take another look at the table contrasting the world's financial priorities with God's priorities. How does the world's thinking lead to overspending?

4. How will incorporating God's priorities bring you financial contentment?

PLAN YOUR SPENDING

LIVING ON PURPOSE . . . . 10 MINUTES

Fellowship

And in him you too are being built together to become a dwelling in which God lives by his Spirit. (Ephesians 2:22 NIV)

The only way a financial plan can help you is if you implement it. Over the next weeks, we're going to be working on tools to help you do that.

In the past, we may have tried to manage our money on our own—with little success. God wants us to find strength to follow our plan to victory through fellowship. True biblical fellowship is more than just snacks and conversation. It invites people into our lives to share our deepest burdens. As the verse from Ephesians tells us, God is building us *together* into a dwelling for his spirit.

Asking someone else to walk with us in this place may seem uncomfortable at first, but we soon discover that a spiritual partner helps us persevere. A spiritual partner holds us up in prayer, and holds us accountable to God. This companion in Christ listens to us, encourages our spiritual growth, and helps us follow through on our commitments. We don't expect any of you to be experts, or you would not be going through this study. The goal of spiritual partnership is support, understanding, accountability, and prayer.

Take some time to select someone in your group to be your spiritual partner for the remaining weeks of this study. We strongly recommend men partner with men, and women partner with women.

PRAYER DIRECTION . . . . 10 MINUTES

Focus your prayers on asking for God's guidance in establishing your spending priorities. Then pray for each other's prayer requests.

PUTTING IT INTO PRACTICE

Complete these assignments before your next meeting.

1. Identifying and writing down your financial goals helps you accomplish what is important to you. Turn to the *Financial Goals* section on the following pages and complete the worksheets. If you are married, we recommend that you and your spouse individually write down your financial goals on separate sheets of paper; then compare goals and compile a complete list on the *Financial Goals* worksheet. Plan to share some of your goals with the group next week. Feedback from others can clarify direction.

2. Please keep recording your expenses. We will need that data in a couple more weeks.

3. Check in with your spiritual partner this week to encourage him or her in thinking through financial goals.

FINANCIAL GOALS

On this worksheet, please go through each category and think about the goals you would like to achieve. Use the sample form as a guide. Record these goals in the appropriate areas, along with the dates you hope to achieve them. Then prioritize your goals.

Pray for the Lord to confirm your goals. Do not allow present circumstances to limit you. Our part is to do what we can as faithful stewards; God's part is to meet our needs and dispense possessions as he sees fit. Some goals may be "faith goals" that you must trust in the Lord to provide. Remember, you don't have to accomplish all your goals at once. For example, until your children are educated you may not be able to save as much as you want for retirement.

Consider discussing some of these goals with your spiritual partner. Encourage each other to take the first steps toward achieving them.

))) PurposeDriven®

FINANCIAL GOALS

CROWN FINANCIAL MINISTRIES

Date: January 1

GIVING GOALS

Would like to give ____15____ percent of my income.

Other giving goals: Contribute $5,000 to world missions over the next 10 years and help support one needy child.

DEBIT REPAYMENT GOALS

Would like to pay off the following debts first:

Creditor	Amount
Sears	$ 100
VISA	$ 900
Crazy Eddie's Auto Sales	$ 4,000
Last National Bank	$ 2,000

EDUCATIONAL GOALS

Would like to fund the following education:

Person	School	Annual Cost	Amount
Johnny	Vo-Tech	$ 8,000	$ 24,000
Ruthie	State College	$ 15,000	$ 60,000
		$	$
		$	$

Other educational goals: Jane would like to study to become a registered nurse.

LIFESTYLE GOALS

Would like to make the following major purchases (home, automobile, appliance):

Item	Amount
Add Porch to Home	$ 8,000
Replace Jane's Car	$ 12,500
Replace Refrigerator	$ 800
	$

Would like to achieve the following annual income: $ 108,000

))) PurposeDriven®

FINANCIAL GOALS, CONT'D

CROWN FINANCIAL MINISTRIES

SAVINGS AND INVESTMENT GOALS

Would like to save _____10_____ percent on my income:

Other savings goals: Increase savings to 15 percent a year within 10 years

Would like to make the following investments:	Investment
Rental property	$15,000 down payment
Retirement account	$4,000 each year
Mutual fund	$3,000 each year

Would like to provide my/our heirs with the following: House and rental property paid for and enough insurance to provide an adequate income to meet their needs

STARTING A BUSINESS

Would like to invest in or begin my/our own business: No

DESCRIBE YOUR STANDARD OF LIVING YOU SENSE WOULD PLEASE THE LORD.

We would be satisfied living in our present home (not moving to a larger or more expensive home). We have the goal of adding a porch on to our home. We want to concentrate on educating our children, paying off our debts, giving more, and saving, rather than increasing our standard of living for the next 15 years. After we have accomplished our financial goals, we want to travel once a year and give one-third of our income. We would like to keep our cars an average of seven years and purchase low-mileage used cars. We want to maintain a simple and more classic wardrobe rather than following the latest clothing fads. We also want to help our children purchase their first home. We want everything we spend to please the Lord.

PurposeDriven®

FINANCIAL GOALS

CROWN FINANCIAL MINISTRIES

Date:

GIVING GOALS

Would like to give _____ percent of my income.

Other giving goals: _____

_____

DEBIT REPAYMENT GOALS

Would like to pay off the following debts first:

Creditor	Amount
	$
	$
	$
	$

EDUCATIONAL GOALS

Would like to fund the following education:

Person	School	Annual Cost	Amount
		$	$
		$	$
		$	$
		$	$

Other educational goals: _____

LIFESTYLE GOALS

Would like to make the following major purchases (home, automobile, appliance):

Item	Amount
	$
	$
	$
	$

Would like to achieve the following annual income: $

PurposeDriven®

FINANCIAL GOALS, CONT'D

CROWN FINANCIAL MINISTRIES

Date:

SAVINGS AND INVESTMENT GOALS

Would like to save _____ percent on my income:

Other savings goals: _____

_____

_____

Would like to make the following investments:	Investment

Would like to provide my/our heirs with the following: _____

_____

STARTING A BUSINESS

Would like to invest in or begin my/our own business: _____

_____

_____

DESCRIBE YOUR STANDARD OF LIVING YOU SENSE WOULD PLEASE THE LORD.

NOTES

3

SESSION THREE

GIVING AS AN ACT OF WORSHIP

CHIP INGRAM

CATCHING UP . . . . 10 MINUTES

- Opening Prayer

- Did you connect with your spiritual partner this week?

- How did the *Financial Goals* exercise go?

- One or two of you share how God is using this study to change your perspective on your finances.

KEY VERSE . . . . 2 MINUTES

> **HOST TIPS:** Ask someone to read aloud the following verse. If anyone has a different translation, ask him or her to read it to expand your understanding of the passage.

You should remember the words of the Lord Jesus:
"It is more blessed to give than to receive."

Acts 20:35b (NLT)

GIVING AS AN ACT OF WORSHIP

 Watch the video lesson now and follow along in your outline. **20** MINUTES

Three Facts about Biblical Generosity:

1. God _____ generous people.

> . . . the Lord Jesus himself said: "It is more blessed to give than to receive." (Acts 20:35b NIV)

> "Give, and it will be given to you. A good measure, pressed down, shaken together and running over, will be poured into your lap. For with the measure you use, it will be measured to you." (Luke 6:38 NIV)

> A generous man will himself be blessed, for he shares his food with the poor. (Proverbs 22:9 NIV)

> He who is kind to the poor lends to the LORD, and he will reward him for what he has done. (Proverbs 19:17 NIV)

Generous giving produces:

- Emotional _____

- Spiritual _____

- Material _____

Where you find a generous nation, a generous family, a generous individual, a generous company or organization, as a general rule you will find blessing and prosperity. God blesses generous people.

2. God provides a _____ for generous people.

Five characteristics of biblical generosity:

a. Biblical generosity gives the _____ and the _____ to God.

> *⁹Honor the LORD with your wealth, with the firstfruits of all your crops; ¹⁰then your barns will be filled to overflowing, and your vats will brim over with new wine.* (Proverbs 3:9–10 NIV)

- The first tenth belongs to God. It's called a _____ .

b. Biblical generosity is _____ and _____ .

> *On the first day of every week, each one of you should set aside a sum of money in keeping with his income, saving it up, so that when I come no collections will have to be made.* (1 Corinthians 16:2 NIV)

We not only give our first and our best to the Lord, we give it regularly and systematically.

c. Biblical generosity is _____ to our income.

Being generous isn't just about percentages. It's also about proportion.

d. Biblical generosity involves _____ .

¹And now, brothers, we want you to know about the grace that God has given the Macedonian churches. ²Out of the most severe trial, their overflowing joy and their extreme poverty welled up in rich generosity. ³For I testify that they gave as much as they were able, and even beyond their ability. Entirely on their own, ⁴they urgently pleaded with us for the privilege of sharing in this service to the saints. (2 Corinthians 8:1–4 NIV)

God measures generosity not just by the amount or the percentage, but also by the depth of sacrifice.

But the king replied to Araunah, "No, I insist on paying you for it. I will not sacrifice to the LORD my God burnt offerings that cost me nothing." (2 Samuel 24:24a NIV)

e. Biblical generosity is thoughtful, voluntary, and _____ .

⁵So I thought it necessary to urge the brothers to visit you in advance and finish the arrangements for the generous gift you had promised. Then it will be ready as a generous gift, not as one grudgingly given. ⁶Remember this: Whoever sows sparingly will also reap sparingly, and whoever sows generously will also reap generously. ⁷Each man should give what he has decided in his heart to give, not reluctantly or under compulsion, for God loves a cheerful giver. (2 Corinthians 9:5–7 NIV)

3. Generosity begins with a _____ .

By faith Abel offered God a better sacrifice than Cain did. By faith he was commended as a righteous man, when God spoke well of his offerings. And by faith he still speaks, even though he is dead. (Hebrews 11:4 NIV)

DISCUSSION QUESTIONS .... 40 MINUTES

1. What were your initial thoughts about a message on giving? If this presentation has changed your mind, share that with the group.

2. When it comes to generous giving, what does it mean to give the first and best to God? What would that look like in your life?

3. Giving is an area that often produces great confusion. How are our attitudes toward giving influenced by our past experiences, and how is sound advice often filtered out by those previous experiences or thinking?

4. Chip said that tithing is not the finish line, it's the starting line. What is the difference between tithing and proportional giving? Why is this an important principle to learn?

5. Describe the hearts of the believers in 2 Corinthians 8:1–4. What were they eager to do, in spite of their meager financial capabilities? Have you ever given sacrificially? Share your story with your group as an encouragement to them.

GIVING AS AN ACT OF WORSHIP

LIVING ON PURPOSE . . . . 10 MINUTES

Worship

You can give without worshiping, but you cannot worship without giving—giving your praise, your love, your time, and your resources from a genuine heart of gratitude. Jesus said in Matthew 15:8–9a (NLT), *8"These people honor me with their lips, but their hearts are far away. 9aTheir worship is a farce . . ."* Obviously, God cares about our giving. He is concerned not simply *that* we give, but *why* we give.

What about you? What is the condition of your heart when it comes to worshiping God with the fruits of your life? When you give, are you doing it out of obligation—a sense of duty—or from a heart overflowing with joy and gratitude for what God has given you? Consider carefully what Jesus said: Worship that doesn't come from the heart is just religious activity.

When you work for a paycheck, you are literally trading your life for money. The ultimate form of Christian worship is a life given to God. Why is giving back to God financially so important to our spiritual growth? As a group, respond to this question and discuss these thoughts on worshiping God through giving.

PRAYER DIRECTION . . . . 10 MINUTES

1. Ask God to search your heart and help you see clearly what currently motivates your giving—or what keeps you from giving. Only when we face the truth about ourselves can we fully surrender to God's desires. Surrender is our true position of worship.

2. If giving is new to you, ask God for courage to take this step of faith. If you are a practiced giver, ask God to take you to a new level. Ask him to increase your spirit of generosity.

Putting It into Practice

Complete these assignments before your next meeting.

1. This week we are going to put together a *Spending Plan*. There are two steps to completing this. First, fill out the *Monthly Income & Priority Expenses* page; then proceed to the *Spending Plan* worksheet. You will find directions for these worksheets on the following pages, or you can use the worksheets on the Resource CD. This exercise will take some time, so please plan accordingly.

2. Don't forget to check in with your spiritual partner again this week to keep yourselves on track with these plans.

Monthly Income & Priority Expenses

First, record your monthly income before all deductions in the "Monthly Income" section at the top.

Note on Variable Income: If some or all of your income consists of commissions or other fluctuating sources, make a conservative estimate for a year and divide by twelve to compute your average monthly income. If this is the case for you, it is very important that you work to establish a savings reserve from which you can draw a steady income. For example, assume a family has a reserve of $5,000 and they plan to spend $4,000 a month. If they earn $3,000 during the month, they would withdraw $1,000 from the savings reserve to meet their plan. If they earn $6,000 in the next month, they would spend only the $4,000 they have planned and deposit the $2,000 into the savings reserve. The biggest challenge for those with unpredictable income is to save the reserve and not spend everything they earn during a high-income month.

Next, determine how much you give, pay in taxes, save, and invest. These are the portions of your gross income that you cannot spend on living expenses.

Tithing/Giving: Include all that you give to your local church, additional Kingdom ministries, and other charities. If there are some gifts you give annually, calculate an average monthly amount by dividing that number by twelve.

Taxes: Deduct federal and state withholdings, Social Security and Medicare, and local taxes from gross income. Beware of the temptation to treat unpaid tax money as money you can spend. Other non-tax deductions will be listed on the *Spending Plan* page, so do not enter them here.

Savings: List all regular saving. Make sure you allocate something here, because a savings account can be used as an emergency fund and is crucial for good planning.

Investments: This is where you have the opportunity to invest toward your long-term financial goals. As you begin to work on your *Spending Plan* in the coming weeks, hopefully you will be able to allocate more toward this category.

» PurposeDriven®   **MONTHLY INCOME & PRIORITY EXPENSES**   CROWN FINANCIAL MINISTRIES
(Add totals on this page to the "Spending Plan" page)

Name: John and Jane Sample

Date: January 1

Monthly Income			
Monthly Salary #1	$ 3,600.00		
Monthly Salary #2	$ 2,500.00		
Interest Income	$ 5.75		
Dividends	$		
Commissions	$		
Bonuses / Tips	$		
Retirement Income #1	$		
Retirement Income #2	$		
Net Business Income	$		
Other Income	$		
GROSS MONTHLY INCOME	Amount	$ 6,105.75	

Priority Expenses			
The Local Church	$ 610.00		
The Poor	$ 50.00		
Other Ministries	$ 10.00		
Other Giving	$		
Tithing/Giving (Monthly)	Amount	$ 670.00	

Federal	$ 509.00		
Medicare	$ 88.45		
Social Security (FICA)	$ 378.20		
State	$ 149.85		
Local	$		
Other	$		
Other	$		
Taxes (Monthly)	Amount	$ 1,125.50	

Savings Account #1	$ 100.00		
Savings Account #2	$ -		
Credit Union #1	$ -		
Credit Union #2	$ -		
Other	$ -		
Savings (Monthly)	Amount	$ 100.00	

401K / 403b Plans	$ 200.00		
College Funds	$ -		
Stock, Bonds, Mutual Funds	$ -		
Real Estate	$ -		
Other	$ -		
Investments (Monthly)	Amount	$ 200.00	

$ 4,010.25

PurposeDriven®

MONTHLY INCOME & PRIORITY EXPENSES

CROWN FINANCIAL MINISTRIES

(Add totals on this page to the "Spending Plan" page)

Name:

Date:

Monthly Income			
Monthly Salary #1	$		
Monthly Salary #2	$		
Interest Income	$		
Dividends	$		
Commissions	$		
Bonuses / Tips	$		
Retirement Income #1	$		
Retirement Income #2	$		
Net Business Income	$		
Other Income	$		
GROSS MONTHLY INCOME	Amount	$	

Priority Expenses			
The Local Church	$		
The Poor	$		
Other Ministries	$		
Other Giving	$		
Tithing/Giving (Monthly)	Amount	$	

Federal	$		
Medicare	$		
Social Security (FICA)	$		
State	$		
Local	$		
Other	$		
Other	$		
Taxes (Monthly)	Amount	$	

Savings Account #1	$		
Savings Account #2	$		
Credit Union #1	$		
Credit Union #2	$		
Other	$		
Savings (Monthly)	Amount	$	

401K / 403b Plans	$		
College Funds	$		
Stock, Bonds, Mutual Funds	$		
Real Estate	$		
Other	$		
Investments (Monthly)	Amount	$	

$

SPENDING PLAN

The purpose of a spending plan is to tell your money where you want it to go, rather than wondering where it went. This is one of the most important worksheets in the entire study, and for many it can be difficult. You may not know what you are spending, or you may be frustrated by what your spending plan reveals. Please be encouraged in knowing there is hope. You are not alone. As you work through this study, you will refine your *Spending Plan* and learn how to make it work.

You should be able to fill in the gray boxes at the top of the page from the numbers you have already computed on the *Personal Financial Profile* and *Monthly Income & Priority Expenses* pages. Your "Net Spendable Income" is calculated by subtracting your giving, taxes, savings, investments, and debt repayment amounts from your gross income. The rest of the sheet will be focused on your living expenses, which are divided into six main categories.

Housing: This category includes all monthly expenses necessary to operate the home, including mortgage or rent payments, taxes, insurance, utilities, and maintenance, as well as furnishings you plan to purchase or improvements you plan to make. If you cannot establish an accurate number for maintenance, use 10% of your monthly mortgage payment.

Transportation: Include automobile payments, insurance, gas, oil, maintenance, tolls, parking, licensing fees, taxes, repairs, etc. For replacement cost, make sure you are allocating enough to account for the eventual replacement of your vehicles. If replacement funds are not currently available, make sure you allocate at least enough for reasonable repairs and set it aside to avoid a crisis later.

Insurance: Insurance premiums for life, health, dental, and disability insurance. Do not include insurance costs associated with the home or automobiles.

Household/Personal: Include groceries, clothing, gifts, beauty supplies, etc. For items like clothing and gifts, estimate the annual amount and divide by twelve. These categories are often underestimated.

Medical/Family/Professional: Include deductibles and co-pays, eyeglasses, prescriptions, dentist, etc. Use a yearly average and divide by twelve.

Entertainment/Recreation: Include vacations, camping trips, membership dues, sporting equipment, hobby expenses, sports events, pets, books, and videos. Also, make sure to include eating out and lunches not brought from home. This category is often the easiest to cut expenses from, but it requires serious decisions and behavior changes to do so.

At the bottom right side of the page, add the six Living Expenses categories together and enter the total in the "Total Expenses" box. Then fill in the "Net Spendable Income" box with the number in the "Net Spendable Income" box at the top of the page. Subtract the "Total Expenses" from the "Net Spendable Income" to calculate your "Variance." If your variance is a negative number, your expenses are greater than your income. You will need to find ways to reduce spending in order to make it balance. If you have a positive variance, you can increase the values in your spending, savings, and investing categories. You must continue working through your *Spending Plan* to balance your Income versus Expenses until you generate a "Variance" amount of $0.00.

PurposeDriven®

SPENDING PLAN

CROWN FINANCIAL MINISTRIES

Name: John and Jane Sample

Date: January 1

For annual expenses, please divide by twelve and enter a monthly amount.

From Monthly Income & Priority Expense pages

GROSS MONTHLY INCOME	$ 6,105.75
TITHING / GIVING	$ 670.00
TAXES	$ 1,125.50
SAVINGS	$ 100.00
INVESTMENTS	$ 200.00
DEBT REPAYMENT (from Personal Financial Statement)	$ 344.36
NET SPENDABLE INCOME	$ 3,665.89

HOUSING

Mortgage / Rent	$ 1,200.89
Taxes	$ 250.00
Home Insurance	$ 50.00
Association Dues	$ -
Additional Real Estate Loan	$ -
Home Maintenance	$ 100.00
Electrical	$ 45.00
Gas	$ 35.00
Water	$ 25.00
Garbage	$ 18.00
Telephone	$ 35.00
Cell Phone	$ 55.00
Furnishings	$ 25.00
Internet Service	$ 25.00
Other	$ -
Other	$ -
TOTAL	$ 1,863.89

TRANSPORTATION

Car Payment	$ 198.00
Car Payment	$ -
Car Payment	$ -
Auto Insurance	$ 91.67
License / Registration	$ 8.00
Gas and Oil	$ 100.00
Auto Maintenance	$ 91.67
Auto Replacement Fund	$ -
Other (tolls/parking/transit fares)	$ -
Other	$ -
TOTAL	$ 489.33

INSURANCE

Life Insurance	$ 31.67
Health Insurance	$ 122.00
Dental Insurance	$ 30.00
Disability Insurance	$ 20.00
Other	$ -
TOTAL	$ 203.67

HOUSEHOLD / PERSONAL

Food / Groceries / Toiletries	$ 350.00
Beauty / Barber	$ 40.00
Laundry / Dry Cleaning	$ 15.00
Books / Subscriptions	$ 66.67
Gifts	$ 83.33
Clothing (Adult and Children)	$ 20.00
Education / Tuition / School Supplies	$ 50.00
Lessons / Tutoring	$ -
Allowance	$ -
Child Support	$ -
Other	$ -
TOTAL	$ 625.00

MEDICAL / FAMILY / PROFESSIONAL

Child Care	-
Medical / Dental / Vision	41.67
Prescription / Glasses / Contacts	22.00
Legal	-
Counseling	-
Profession Dues / Memberships	-
Other	
Other	
Other	
TOTAL	$ 63.67

ENTERTAINMENT / RECREATION

Dining Out	75.00
Lunch / Snacks	60.00
Movies / Events	40.00
Baby-sitting	40.00
Vacation / Trips	83.33
Cable TV	35.00
Books / Subscriptions	10.00
Health Club / Hobbies	12.00
Pets	15.00
Cash	50.00
Other	-
TOTAL	$ 420.33

TOTAL EXPENSES	$ 6,105.75
GROSS INCOME (from above)	$ 6,105.75
VARIANCE	$ -

Managing Finances God's Way – Practical Application Worksheet

PurposeDriven®

SPENDING PLAN

CROWN FINANCIAL MINISTRIES

Name: _____

Date: _____

For annual expenses, please divide by twelve and enter a monthly amount.

From Monthly Income & Priority Expense pages

GROSS MONTHLY INCOME	$
TITHING / GIVING	$
TAXES	$
SAVINGS	$
INVESTMENTS	$
DEBT REPAYMENT (from Personal Financial Statement)	$
NET SPENDABLE INCOME	$

HOUSING

Mortgage / Rent	$
Taxes	$
Home Insurance	$
Association Dues	$
Additional Real Estate Loan	$
Home Maintenance	$
Electrical	$
Gas	$
Water	$
Garbage	$
Telephone	$
Cell Phone	$
Furnishings	$
Internet Service	$
Other	$
Other	$
TOTAL	$

TRANSPORTATION

Car Payment	$
Car Payment	$
Car Payment	$
Auto Insurance	$
License / Registration	$
Gas and Oil	$
Auto Maintenance	$
Auto Replacement Fund	$
Other (tolls/parking/transit fares)	$
Other	$
TOTAL	$

INSURANCE

Life Insurance	$
Health Insurance	$
Dental Insurance	$
Disability Insurance	$
Other	$
TOTAL	$

HOUSEHOLD / PERSONAL

Food / Groceries / Toiletries	$
Beauty / Barber	$
Laundry / Dry Cleaning	$
Books / Subscriptions	$
Gifts	$
Clothing (Adult and Children)	$
Education / Tuition / School Supplies	$
Lessons / Tutoring	$
Allowance	$
Child Support	$
Other	$
TOTAL	$

MEDICAL / FAMILY / PROFESSIONAL

Child Care	
Medical / Dental / Vision	
Prescription / Glasses / Contacts	
Legal	
Counseling	
Profession Dues / Memberships	
Other	
Other	
Other	
TOTAL	$

ENTERTAINMENT / RECREATION

Dining Out	
Lunch / Snacks	
Movies / Events	
Baby-sitting	
Vacation / Trips	
Cable TV	
Books / Subscriptions	
Health Club / Hobbies	
Pets	
Cash	
Other	
TOTAL	$

TOTAL EXPENSES	$
NET SPENDABLE INCOME (from 1st column above)	$
VARIANCE	$

NOTES

SESSION FOUR

SAVING AND INVESTING

RON BLUE

CATCHING UP . . . . 10 MINUTES

- Opening Prayer

- How did the truth you learned about giving in our last session impact your life this past week?

- How did the *Spending Plan* go? Were you able to get it to balance out? One or two people briefly share your experiences with the group.

KEY VERSE . . . . 2 MINUTES

> **HOST TIPS:** Ask someone to read aloud the following verse. If anyone has a different translation, ask him or her to read it to expand your understanding of the passage.

*The servant to whom he had entrusted
the five bags of gold said,
"Sir, you gave me five bags of gold to invest,
and I have doubled the amount." The master was full
of praise. "Well done, my good and faithful servant.
You have been faithful in handling this small amount,
so now I will give you many more responsibilities.
Let's celebrate together!"*

Matthew 25:20–21 (NLT)

SAVING AND INVESTING

 Watch the video lesson now and follow along in your outline. . . . . **25** MINUTES

There is no such thing as a perfect investment!

> *A faithful man will be richly blessed, but one eager to get rich will not go unpunished.* (Proverbs 28:20 NIV)

> *The trustworthy will get a rich reward. But the person who wants to get rich quick will only get into trouble.* (Proverbs 28:20 NLT)

PRINCIPLE: The world says, "Get rich quick." The Bible says, "Get rich slow."

> *"Suppose one of you wants to build a tower. Will he not first sit down and estimate the cost to see if he has enough money to complete it?"* (Luke 14:28 NIV)

PRINCIPLE: Take a long-term perspective on all of your investment decisions.

> *¹³I have seen a grievous evil under the sun: wealth hoarded to the harm of its owner, ¹⁴or wealth lost through some misfortune, so that when he has a son there is nothing left for him.* (Ecclesiastes 5:13–14 NIV)

PRINCIPLE: The world's priority: spend and consume first.
Biblical priority: save and invest first.

> *⁶Go to the ant, you sluggard; consider its ways and be wise! ⁷It has no commander, no overseer or ruler, ⁸yet it stores its provisions in summer and gathers its food at harvest.* (Proverbs 6:6–8 NIV)

PRINCIPLE: The world's perspective: time is the enemy . . . "I want it now!"
Biblical perspective: time is a tool . . . start saving now for the future.

> *Divide your portion to seven, or even to eight, for you do not know what misfortune may occur on the earth.* (Ecclesiastes 11:2 NASB)

PRINCIPLE: The world says, "I can always buy low and sell high."
The Bible says, "Diversify, diversify, diversify!"

- Wealth is typically _____ by a career or vocation over a long time frame.

- Wealth is _____ by a diversified investment strategy. Why diversity? Because it is impossible to predict the future of any investment.

THE RULE OF 72

How long will it take to double your money at any given growth rate? The Rule of 72 tells you that if you divide the rate of growth into 72 you will get your answer. Look at this example.

Let's say you make a one-time investment of $1,000 in a savings account that pays 3% per year. The Rule of 72 tells you to divide 3 (the growth rate) into 72. The answer is 24. Therefore, at 3% your original investment of $1,000 will double to $2,000 in 24 years.

If the investment pays 6% per year, the Rule of 72 tells you to divide 6 (the growth rate) into 72. The answer is 12. Therefore, at 6% your original investment of $1,000 will double every 12 years. It will double to $2,000 in 12 years, and it will double again to $4,000 in 24 years.

If the investment pays 12% per year, the Rule of 72 tells you to divide 12 (the growth rate) into 72. The answer is 6. Therefore, at 12% your original investment of $1,000 will double every six years. It will double to $2,000 in 6 years, and it will double again to $4,000 in 12 years. It will double a third time to $8,000 in 18 years, and it will double a fourth time to $16,000 in 24 years.

In other words, in the same 24 year period, your original $1,000 investment will grow to $2,000 at 3% per year, to $4,000 at 6% per year, or to $16,000 at 12% per year.

Growth Rate	Rule of 72	6 years	12 years	18 years	24 years
$1,000 @ 3%	72/3 = 24 years to double				$ 2,000.00
$1,000 @ 6%	72/6 = 12 years to double		$ 2,000.00		$ 4,000.00
$1,000 @ 12%	72/12 = 6 years to double	$ 2,000.00	$ 4,000.00	$ 8,000.00	$ 16,000.00

THE MAGIC OF COMPOUNDING

Interest earns interest, which earns interest, which earns interest—it has a compounding impact on your investment. Look at the following charts:

Chart 1: Compounding a one-time investment of $10,000 over 40 years

	End of Year Values							
	5	10	15	20	25	30	35	40
2%	11,041	12,190	13,459	14,859	16,406	18,114	19,999	22,080
4%	12,167	14,802	18,009	21,911	26,658	32,434	39,461	48,010
6%	13,382	17,908	23,966	32,071	42,919	57,435	76,861	102,857
8%	14,693	21,589	31,722	46,610	68,485	100,627	147,853	217,245
10%	16,105	25,937	41,772	67,275	108,347	174,494	281,024	452,593
12%	17,623	31,058	54,736	96,463	170,001	299,599	527,996	930,510
14%	19,254	37,072	71,379	137,435	264,619	509,502	981,002	1,888,835
16%	21,003	44,114	92,655	194,608	408,742	858,499	1,803,141	3,787,212
18%	22,878	52,338	119,737	273,930	626,686	1,433,706	3,279,973	7,503,783
20%	24,883	61,917	154,070	383,376	953,962	2,373,763	5,906,682	14,697,716

Chart 2: Compounding $1,000 invested per year over 40 years

	End of Year Values							
	5	10	15	20	25	30	35	40
2%	5,204	10,950	17,293	24,297	32,030	40,568	49,994	60,402
4%	5,416	12,006	20,024	29,778	41,646	56,085	73,652	95,026
6%	5,637	13,181	23,276	36,786	54,865	79,058	111,435	154,762
8%	5,867	14,487	27,152	45,762	73,106	113,283	172,317	259,057
10%	6,105	15,937	31,772	57,275	98,347	164,494	271,024	442,593
12%	6,353	17,549	37,280	72,052	133,334	241,333	431,663	767,091
14%	6,610	19,337	43,842	91,025	181,871	356,787	693,573	1,342,025
16%	6,877	21,321	51,660	115,380	249,214	530,312	1,120,713	2,360,757
18%	7,154	23,521	60,965	146,628	342,603	790,948	1,816,652	4,163,213
20%	7,442	25,959	72,035	186,688	471,981	1,181,882	2,948,341	7,343,858

Because of the magic of compounding, you don't have to *earn* a lot to *make* a lot if you start early.

Saving and investing is a high priority. Saving and investing allows you to meet your long-term financial goals.

The Opportunity Cost of Consumption

When you spend money on consumption, it costs you not only the money you spend, but the potential money you could have earned if you had invested instead.

Let's say, for example, that you saved $1,000 per year, or $83.33 per month every year for 40 years. According to Chart 2, at 8% growth over 40 years that money would grow to $259,000. If, on the other hand, you spent that $1,000 each year, or $83.33 each month, after 40 years it would cost you not just $40,000, but the $259,000 you could have earned if you had invested the money instead.

Prioritizing Your Investment Decisions

There is a sequence to making good investments:

Step 1: Pay off _____ debt.

Step 2: Set money aside for an _____ .

Step 3: Save for _____ .

Step 4: Diversify your investments to meet _____ .

Step 5: Begin taking calculated financial _____ .

Before you invest, ask yourself:

• What are my reasons for making this investment? Is it to provide for my family? Is it to meet a future need?

• What is my attitude toward this investment? Am I driven by greed or pride or fear? Or am I driven by a long-term strategy?

• Am I presuming upon the future?

- Will I create anxiety by making this investment? Never invest beyond the point that you can sleep!

- How does my spouse feel about this investment? A husband and wife need to be in total unity on their investments.

Look for _____ to make your investment decisions.

> *Plans fail for lack of counsel, but with many advisers they succeed.*
> (Proverbs 15:22 NIV)

HOST TIP: Please note that times for these sections are different in this lesson to allow appropriate time for discussion.

DISCUSSION QUESTIONS . . . . .25 MINUTES

1. What did you hear in this lesson that changed the way you think about saving and investing?

2. Discuss any fears or frustrations you have experienced when it comes to saving or investing for the future.

3. Does anyone in the group have a story to share about a world perspective that led to financial problems in your life? What lessons did you learn?

LIVING ON PURPOSE . . . . 25 MINUTES

Discipleship

Biblical stewardship is a big part of discipleship. In teaching his disciples, Jesus told the parable of the talents. Take a moment to look at that parable now, in Matthew 25:14–30. Discuss it in light of the Rule of 72, the Magic of Compounding, and the Opportunity Cost of Consumption.

• How did the wise servants practice these principles?

• How are those who choose to live as wise servants exemplifying Christ like character?

• Like the man in the parable who went on the journey, God has entrusted his property to you. Will you be like the man who buried his master's money, or will you put it to work in order to grow it for God?

• What can you give up today in order to invest for tomorrow?

PRAYER DIRECTION . . . . 10 MINUTES

Saving and investing can require that we make difficult decisions and restructure our priorities. Pray for each other that God will give us courage, wisdom, and peace of mind (and in our households!) as we make choices that enable us to save and invest wisely.

PUTTING IT INTO PRACTICE

Complete these assignments before your next meeting.

1. Last week you developed a spending plan, and over the last four weeks you have been tracking your financial transactions. This week you will enter these transactions into a *Monthly Expenses* worksheet. You will find an example of this worksheet along with detailed instructions on the following pages and on the Resource CD.

2. Once that is complete, you will begin to see how you are doing relative to your *Spending Plan*. This is where you may have to make some difficult decisions about where you really want your money to go. Are you going to stick to the plan, or will you let it slip?

   All too often we are tripped up by the natural desire to avoid work, or put it off for later. But without this type of determined planning and decision making, the reality is we probably won't reach our financial goals.

3. Please continue to record all your financial transactions on your pad, and check in with your spiritual partner this week to encourage him or her to make good financial choices.

NOTES

MONTHLY EXPENSES WORKSHEET

The *Monthly Expenses* worksheets are provided for you to record your daily and monthly spending for each individual month. First, enter the month and year at the top.

Across the top of the worksheet, you see the fields to record your income and spending by category. On the left side of the worksheet are the days of the month so you can record your daily income and spending for your specific category accounts. Enter the spending transactions you have been recording over the last several weeks into this sheet. When you have completely entered all of your transactions for the month, add up the individual columns and enter the total into the "This Month Actual" areas at the bottom. This will tell you how much you actually spent in each category for the month, so you can compare these numbers with your *Spending Plan*. Then add the totals and enter your "Total Expenses" to the right. Did you have more income than expenses this month?

From now on, enter your spending transactions into the *Monthly Expenses* worksheet each week. Whether you spend by cash, check, or credit card, enter your transactions into the proper categories right away. Then, any time during the month that you want to buy an item, you can look at what you have already spent for the month in that category and compare it to the planned amount. We recommend that midway through the month you total what you have spent so far for every category on the line titled "This Month Subtotal," to help you monitor your spending.

Now you will need to go back and adjust and rebalance your *Spending Plan*. The best way to do this is to review each income and spending category. Can you think of any ways to increase your income? Then ask yourself two questions about each spending category: Do I really need this? If so, can I purchase it less expensively? Some of the decisions will be difficult to make. It is not easy to reduce spending. It may be necessary to consider a change in housing, automobiles, personal habits, or dining out. But the freedom that comes from balancing your *Spending Plan*, getting out of debt, giving more generously, and funding your financial goals is worth the sacrifice.

Did you have a surplus at the end of the month? Don't think that you automatically have extra money to spend. You will need to have a surplus for several months in order to meet expenses that are annual, such as automobile insurance, real estate taxes, etc. Enter these in full as they occur. These categories will even out over time.

When you finish reviewing your expenses at the end of each month, review your plan and decide if it needs adjustments. We pray that you will establish the long-term habit of planning and managing your expenses to gain financial stability and reach your financial goals.

PurposeDriven

MONTHLY EXPENSES

CROWN FINANCIAL MINISTRIES

Month: **January**   Year:

Category	GROSS INCOME	TITHE/GIVING	TAXES	Savings	Investments	Debt Repayment	Housing
PLANNED AMOUNT	$6,105.75	$670.00	$1,125.50	$100.00	$200.00	344.36	$1,863.89
Date							
1	3,050.00		562.75	25.00	100.00	120.00	1,200.89
2						100.00	
3							
4		305.00					
5							
6							
7							
8							
9							
10							
11							
12							
13							
14							
15	3,050.00		562.75	25.00	100.00		
This month SUBTOTAL	$6,100.00	$305.00	$1,125.50	$50.00	$200.00	220.00	$1,200.89
16						124.36	
17		305.00					
18							
19							70.00
20							25.00
21							20.00
22							22.00
23							35.00
24							90.00
25							30.00
26		50.00					
27							
28							
29							
30							
31							
This month ACTUAL	$6,100.00	660.00	$1,125.50	50.00	200.00	344.36	$1,492.89
This month vs. PLAN	$(5.75)	10.00	-	50.00	-	-	371.00
Year to Date PLAN	$6,105.75	670.00	$1,125.50	100.00	200.00	344.36	$1,863.89
Year to Date ACTUAL	$6,100.00	660.00	$1,125.50	50.00	200.00	344.36	$1,492.89
Year to Date ACTUAL vs. PLAN	$(5.75)	10.00	-	50.00	-	-	371.00

SPENDING SUMMARY

This Month		Previous Month / Year to Date		Year to Date
Total Gross Income $6,100.00		Total Gross Income $ -		Total Gross Income $6,100.00
Minus Total Expenses $5,749.30	**+**	Minus Total Expenses $ -	**=**	Minus Total Expenses $5,749.30
Equals Surplus/Deficit $350.70		Equals Surplus/Deficit $ -		Equals Surplus/Deficit $350.70

PurposeDriven

MONTHLY EXPENSES

CROWN FINANCIAL MINISTRIES

Category	Transportation	Insurance	Household/ Personal	Medical/Family/ Professional	Entertainment/ Recreation	TOTAL EXPENSES	This Month SURPLUS/ DEFICIT
PLANNED AMOUNT	$ 489.33	$ 203.67	$ 625.00	$ 63.67	$ 420.33	$6,105.75	$ -
Date							
1	198.00	172.00	100.00			$2,478.64	$ 571.36
2		31.67	25.00		52.50	$ 209.17	$ 362.19
3					12.00	$ 12.00	$ 350.19
4			26.85		50.00	$ 381.85	$ (31.66)
5			50.00			$ 50.00	$ (81.66)
6	28.00		68.00		5.25	$ 101.25	$ (182.91)
7					4.83	$ 4.83	$ (187.74)
8			30.00			$ 30.00	$ (217.74)
9					36.93	$ 36.93	$ (254.67)
10			20.00			$ 20.00	$ (274.67)
11			25.50		4.29	$ 29.79	$ (304.46)
12				20.00	5.76	$ 25.76	$ (330.22)
13					3.67	$ 3.67	$ (333.89)
14			106.00			$ 106.00	$ (439.89)
15			15.75			$ 703.50	$1,906.61
This month SUBTOTAL	$ 226.00	$ 203.67	$ 467.10	$ 20.00	$ 175.23	$4,193.39	$1,906.61
16	100.00		20.00		52.26	$ 296.62	$1,609.99
17			44.97			$ 349.97	$1,260.02
18	31.00			40.00		$ 71.00	$1,189.02
19			98.75		32.79	$ 201.54	$ 987.48
20					4.61	$ 29.61	$ 957.87
21			22.75		6.82	$ 49.57	$ 908.30
22			121.36			$ 143.36	$ 764.94
23					72.35	$ 107.35	$ 657.59
24						$ 90.00	$ 567.59
25					5.25	$ 35.25	$ 532.34
26					6.14	$ 56.14	$ 476.20
27			28.65		9.33	$ 37.98	$ 438.22
28	33.00			20.00	3.99	$ 56.99	$ 381.23
29						$ -	$ 381.23
30			30.53			$ 30.53	$ 350.70
31						$ -	$ 350.70
This month ACTUAL	$ 390.00	$ 203.67	$ 834.11	$ 80.00	$ 368.77	$5,749.30	$ 350.70
This month vs. PLAN	$ 99.33	$ (0.00)	$ (209.11)	$ (16.33)	$ 51.56	$ 356.45	$ 350.70
Year to Date PLAN	$ 489.33	$ 203.67	$ 625.00	$ 63.67	$ 420.33	$6,105.75	$ -
Year to Date ACTUAL	$ 390.00	$ 203.67	$ 834.11	$ 80.00	$ 368.77	$5,749.30	$ 350.70
Year to Date ACTUAL vs. PLAN	$ 99.33	$ (0.00)	$ (209.11)	$ (16.33)	$ 51.56	$ 356.45	$ 350.70

PurposeDriven®

MONTHLY EXPENSES

CROWN FINANCIAL MINISTRIES

Month: _____ **Year:** _____

Category	GROSS INCOME	TITHE/GIVING	TAXES	Savings	Investments	Debt Repayment	Housing
PLANNED AMOUNT	$	$	$	$	$	$	$
Date							
1							
2							
3							
4							
5							
6							
7							
8							
9							
10							
11							
12							
13							
14							
15							
This month SUBTOTAL	$	$	$	$	$	$	$
16							
17							
18							
19							
20							
21							
22							
23							
24							
25							
26							
27							
28							
29							
30							
31							
This month ACTUAL	$	$	$	$	$	$	$
This month vs. PLAN	$	$	$	$	$	$	$
Year to Date PLAN	$	$	$	$	$	$	$
Year to Date ACTUAL	$	$	$	$	$	$	$
Year to Date ACTUAL vs. PLAN	$	$	$	$	$	$	$

SPENDING SUMMARY

This Month		Previous Month / Year to Date		Year to Date
Total Gross Income $_____		Total Gross Income $_____		Total Gross Income $_____
Minus Total Expenses $_____	**+**	Minus Total Expenses $_____	**=**	Minus Total Expenses $_____
Equals Surplus/Deficit $_____		Equals Surplus/Deficit $_____		Equals Surplus/Deficit $_____

>>> PurposeDriven®

MONTHLY EXPENSES

CROWN FINANCIAL MINISTRIES

Category	Transportation	Insurance	Household/ Personal	Medical/Family/ Professional	Entertainment/ Recreation	TOTAL EXPENSES	This Month SURPLUS/ DEFICIT
PLANNED AMOUNT	$	$	$	$	$	$	$
Date							
1						$	$
2						$	$
3						$	$
4						$	$
5						$	$
6						$	$
7						$	$
8						$	$
9						$	$
10						$	$
11						$	$
12						$	$
13						$	$
14						$	$
15						$	$
This month SUBTOTAL	$	$	$	$	$	$	$
16						$	$
17						$	$
18						$	$
19						$	$
20						$	$
21						$	$
22						$	$
23						$	$
24						$	$
25						$	$
26						$	$
27						$	$
28						$	$
29						$	$
30						$	$
31						$	$
This month ACTUAL	$	$	$	$	$	$	$
This month vs. PLAN	$	$	$	$	$	$	$
Year to Date PLAN	$	$	$	$	$	$	$
Year to Date ACTUAL	$	$	$	$	$	$	$
Year to Date ACTUAL vs. PLAN	$	$	$	$	$	$	$

NOTES

SESSION FIVE

GOD'S SOLUTION TO DEBT

HOWARD DAYTON

CATCHING UP . . . . 10 MINUTES

- Opening Prayer

- Did you connect with your spiritual partner this week?

- How did it go with the *Monthly Expenses* worksheet? Were you able to complete it and compare it to your *Spending Plan* from the previous week? One or two of you share what you learned.

- Did you make any difficult decisions that you will need encouragement and prayer to implement?

KEY VERSE . . . . 2 MINUTES

> **HOST TIPS:** Ask someone to read aloud the following verse. If anyone has a different translation, ask him or her to read it to expand your understanding of the passage.

Let no debt remain outstanding,
except the continuing debt to love one another,
for he who loves his fellowman has fulfilled the law.

Romans 13:8 (NIV)

Watch the video lesson now and follow along in your outline. . . . . **25** MINUTES

Pay all your debts . . . (Romans 13:8a NLT)

Owe nothing to anyone . . . (Romans 13:8a NASB)

Keep out of debt and *owe no man anything* . . . (Romans 13:8a AMP)

. . . *the borrower is servant to the lender.* (Proverbs 22:7b NIV)

When we're in debt, we're in a position of servitude to the lender. And the deeper we're in debt, the more of a servant we become. We don't have the freedom to decide where we spend our money because we've already legally obligated ourselves to pay these debts.

Nine Steps to Becoming Debt-Free

1. _____ .

> *Do not be anxious about anything, but in everything, by prayer and petition, with thanksgiving, present your requests to God.* (Philippians 4:6 NIV)

2. **Develop a** _____ **mind set.**

> *Do not conform any longer to the pattern of this world, but be transformed by the renewing of your mind.* (Romans 12:2a NIV)

3. **List** _____ .

Be sure to write down the interest rate on each debt. It will help you decide which debt to pay off first.

4. List everything _____ .

Is there something you could sell that you are not using? Use the money to pay off debt.

5. Establish a _____ .

A spending plan allows you to ask yourself two important questions:

- Can I do it for less?

- Do I really need it?

6. Establish a _____ schedule.

7. Consider earning _____ .

One caution: the extra work should not be so much that it harms your relationship with the Lord or your family.

8. Consider a radical change in your _____ .

Many people temporarily lower their cost of living to become debt-free.

9. Don't _____ !

And let us not get tired of doing what is right, for after a while we will reap a harvest of blessing if we don't get discouraged and give up.
(Galatians 6:9 LB)

Four Critical Issues

1. How do you decide which debt to pay off first?

Two factors: a) The size of the debts

                  b) The interest rate charged

Focus on paying off the smallest debt first. You'll be encouraged as it's eliminated, and this will free more cash to apply against other debts. Then, after you pay off the first debt, apply its payment toward the next smallest debt. After the second debt is paid off, apply what you were paying on the first and second debts toward the next debt and so forth.

2. Understand your credit score.

Your credit score determines the amount of interest you will pay.

A credit score is a number designed to help lenders measure your likelihood of making timely payments. It's called a FICO score, and it ranges from 300 to 850. The higher your score the better. FICO scores above 700 indicate a good credit risk, while scores below 600 indicate a poor risk.

Your credit score is determined by the information contained in your credit report. Once every twelve months you can check your credit report for free by logging on to www.annualcreditreport.com. At this site you will be able to get a copy of your credit report from each of the nationwide consumer credit reporting companies: Equifax®, Experian®, and TransUnion®. You will also have the option to purchase your credit score for a nominal fee.

You can improve your credit score by paying your bills on time and by reducing your amount of debt.

3. How to escape the auto debt trap.

First, decide in advance to keep your car for at least three years after you've paid it off. Then, continue paying the monthly car payment, but pay it into your own savings account. Finally, when you're ready to replace your car, the saved cash plus the trade-in value of the old car should be enough to buy a good, low-mileage used car without going into debt.

4. Cosigning

A person who cosigns becomes legally responsible for the debt of another person.

A study by the Federal Trade Commission found that fifty percent of those who cosigned for bank loans ended up making the payments. And seventy-five percent of those who cosigned for finance company loans ended up making the payments.

> *It is poor judgment to countersign another's note, to become responsible for his debts.* (Proverbs 17:18 LB)

You Can Do This!

> *". . . with God all things are possible."* (Mark 10:27b KJV)

> *. . . [God] is able to do immeasurably more than all we ask or imagine . . .* (Ephesians 3:20 NIV)

> *I can do all things through Christ who strengthens me.* (Philippians 4:13 NKJV)

> *And let us not get tired of doing what is right, for after a while we will reap a harvest of blessing if we don't get discouraged and give up.* (Galatians 6:9 LB)

DISCUSSION QUESTIONS . . . . 40 MINUTES

1. Why do you think God cares about your debt?

2. Howard shared his own success story about getting out of debt. Does anyone in the group have a similar story they would like to share?

3. Talk about how being in debt makes you feel. How does it affect your home life, your thought life, your relationships? How would all that change if you were debt-free?

4. Take time to discuss any questions about how to pay off debt.

5. No matter what your present FICO score, what encouragement did you find in this lesson for raising it?

LIVING ON PURPOSE . . . . 10 MINUTES

Ministry & Evangelism

No matter how difficult the task of becoming debt-free may seem, the Lord is there to walk you through it. In fact, he has already planned to do this as part of helping you find your ultimate purpose in life. Jesus said, [29]*"Take my yoke upon you and learn from me, for I am gentle and humble in heart, and you will find rest for your souls. *[30]*For my yoke is easy and my burden is light"* (Matthew 11:29–30 NIV).

Even if the light at the end of the tunnel seems a long way off, remember that God wants you out of debt even more than you do. He knows that indebtedness keeps you from being free to help others and hinders the effectiveness of your witness for Christ.

- How would you use your money, to further the Gospel message if you were debt-free?

- How can you use your time, money, and resources to touch people for Christ now?

PRAYER DIRECTION . . . . 10 MINUTES

Commit your debts into God's care. Ask him for guidance in making decisions that will lead you to freedom from indebtedness, as well as for determination to follow through with those decisions.

PUTTING IT INTO PRACTICE

Complete these assignments before your next meeting.

1. On the following pages, you will find an exercise called the *Debt Repayment Schedule*. This will help you determine how long it will take you to pay off your outstanding loans. You can also use the electronic worksheet or the debt eliminator program (DebtElim_Setup.exe) included on your Resource CD, and the calculations will all be done for you automatically. These tools show you how much faster you can pay off a debt if you increase your monthly payments. Using the principles in this session, determine which debts to begin paying off first and create a payment calendar.

2. Talk to your spiritual partner at least once this week, and see if he or she would like prayer support while going through this exercise.

3. Take time this week to visit www.annualcreditreport.com to review your credit reports.

DEBT REPAYMENT SCHEDULE

This worksheet will help you plan your effort to get out of debt. There are several blank *Debt Repayment Schedules* in this workbook, but if you need more, you may photocopy the form. We highly recommend that you use a computer to help you in your calculations. If you are unable to use the Excel worksheets on the Resource CD, try using the Debt Eliminator program. It will run the calculations for you, and it will enable you to easily see how a change in payment will affect the long-term schedule. For example, you might want to see how much more quickly you will able to pay off a debt by increasing your payments. The Debt Eliminator will figure it out for you instantly.

To use the worksheet manually, enter the information on the top of the page: the creditor's name, why the money was borrowed, the total amount still owed, the interest rate being charged, your monthly payment, and the current date. If you do not know how many payments you have left, leave that blank.

Notice there are four columns:

1. **Payment Number:** If you are doing the sheet manually, enter the date each payment is due.

2. **Amount Paid:** The amount you pay each month.

3. **Payments Remaining:** The number of payments you have left. You may want to do this last. Once you have worked down the sheet in the other columns, simply number them up from the bottom. (See sample schedule on adjacent page.)

4. **Balance Due:** Calculate the remaining balance after each payment is made. Don't forget to figure in the interest that is paid with each payment. The tools on the Resource CD will do this for you automatically.

DEBT REPAYMENT SCHEDULE

PurposeDriven®   CROWN FINANCIAL MINISTRIES

CREDITOR:	Care Loan Credit Union	Date:	January 18

Describe What Was Purchased: Toyota Camry

Amount Owed:	$3,500.00	Interest Rate:	5.500%
Total Number of Payments:	19	Monthly Payment:	198.00

Payment Number	Amount Paid	Payments Remaining	Balance Due
1	$ 198.00	19	$ 3,318.04
2	$ 198.00	18	$ 3,135.25
3	$ 198.00	17	$ 2,951.62
4	$ 198.00	16	$ 2,767.15
5	$ 198.00	15	$ 2,581.83
6	$ 198.00	14	$ 2,395.66
7	$ 198.00	13	$ 2,208.64
8	$ 198.00	12	$ 2,020.77
9	$ 198.00	11	$ 1,832.03
10	$ 198.00	10	$ 1,642.43
11	$ 198.00	9	$ 1,451.95
12	$ 198.00	8	$ 1,260.61
13	$ 198.00	7	$ 1,068.39
14	$ 198.00	6	$ 875.28
15	$ 198.00	5	$ 681.29
16	$ 198.00	4	$ 486.42
17	$ 198.00	3	$ 290.65
18	$ 198.00	2	$ 93.98
19	$ 94.41	1	$ -
20	$	0	$ -
21	$		$
22	$		$
23	$		$
24	$		$
25	$		$
26	$		$
27	$		$
28	$		$
29	$		$
30	$		$
31	$		$
32	$		$
33	$		$
34	$		$
35	$		$
36	$		$
37	$		$
38	$		$
39	$		$
40	$		$
41	$		$
42	$		$
43	$		$
44	$		$
45	$		$

PurposeDriven

DEBT REPAYMENT SCHEDULE

CROWN FINANCIAL MINISTRIES

CREDITOR: _____ **Date:** _____

Describe What Was Purchased: _____

Amount Owed: _____ **Interest Rate:** _____

Total Number of Payments: _____ **Monthly Payment:** _____

Payment Number	Amount Paid	Payments Remaining	Balance Due
1	$		$
2	$		$
3	$		$
4	$		$
5	$		$
6	$		$
7	$		$
8	$		$
9	$		$
10	$		$
11	$		$
12	$		$
13	$		$
14	$		$
15	$		$
16	$		$
17	$		$
18	$		$
19	$		$
20	$		$
21	$		$
22	$		$
23	$		$
24	$		$
25	$		$
26	$		$
27	$		$
28	$		$
29	$		$
30	$		$
31	$		$
32	$		$
33	$		$
34	$		$
35	$		$
36	$		$
37	$		$
38	$		$
39	$		$
40	$		$
41	$		$
42	$		$
43	$		$
44	$		$
45	$		$

DEBT REPAYMENT SCHEDULE

PurposeDriven® · CROWN FINANCIAL MINISTRIES

CREDITOR:		**Date:**	
Describe What Was Purchased:			
Amount Owed:		**Interest Rate:**	
Total Number of Payments:		**Monthly Payment:**	

Payment Number	Amount Paid	Payments Remaining	Balance Due
46	$		$
47	$		$
48	$		$
49	$		$
50	$		$
51	$		$
52	$		$
53	$		$
54	$		$
55	$		$
56	$		$
57	$		$
58	$		$
59	$		$
60	$		$
61	$		$
62	$		$
63	$		$
64	$		$
65	$		$
66	$		$
67	$		$
68	$		$
69	$		$
70	$		$
71	$		$
72	$		$
73	$		$
74	$		$
75	$		$
76	$		$
77	$		$
78	$		$
79	$		$
80	$		$
81	$		$
82	$		$
83	$		$
84	$		$
85	$		$
86	$		$
87	$		$
88	$		$
89	$		$
90	$		$

NOTES

6

SESSION SIX

ENJOY WHAT GOD HAS GIVEN YOU

CHUCK BENTLEY

Managing Our Finances

Catching Up . . . . 5 minutes

- Opening Prayer

- At the beginning of this series, we asked how you would live if you were financially free. In light of what you have learned in this study, how would you answer that question today?

- Take a few minutes to discuss how you're doing with your debt repayment schedules. How does it feel to have a plan to pay off your debt?

Key Verse . . . . 2 minutes

> **Host Tips:** Ask someone to read aloud the following verse. If anyone has a different translation, ask him or her to read it to expand your understanding of the passage.

When God gives any man wealth and possessions, and enables him to enjoy them, to accept his lot and be happy in his work—this is a gift of God.

Ecclesiastes 5:19 (NIV)

ENJOY WHAT GOD HAS GIVEN YOU

 Watch the video lesson now and follow along in your outline. . . . . **25** MINUTES

We are God's _____ .

> *O LORD our God, as for all this abundance . . . it comes from your hand, and all of it belongs to you.* (1 Chronicles 29:16 NIV)

Recognizing God's ownership of all things is a threshold moment in our Christian experience. It frees us to take our eyes off the temporal and begin to live with eternity in mind.

God truly wants us to _____ the resources that he has given us.

> *They will celebrate your abundant goodness and joyfully sing of your righteousness.* (Psalm 145:7 NIV)

1. The Lord expects us to take care of _____ .

> *If anyone does not provide for his relatives, and especially for his immediate family, he has denied the faith and is worse than an unbeliever.* (1 Timothy 5:8 NIV)

Taking care of your family is not only a God-given priority, it is a God-given privilege. God wants you to rejoice with your family, and to take every occasion to explain to them the goodness he has shown to you.

2. The Lord wants us to enjoy regular periods of _____

_____ .

It is a testimony to your faith and trust in God as your Provider when you rest from your labors.

> *Six days do your work, but on the seventh day do not work . . .*
> (Exodus 23:12a NIV)

3. The Lord tells us that when we enjoy his blessings, we bring him more

_____ .

> *[18]Then I realized that it is good and proper for a man to eat and drink, and to find satisfaction in his toilsome labor under the sun during the few days of life God has given him—for this is his lot. [19]Moreover, when God gives any man wealth and possessions, and enables him to enjoy them, to accept his lot and be happy in his work—this is a gift of God. [20]He seldom reflects on the days of his life, because God keeps him occupied with gladness of heart.* (Ecclesiastes 5:18–20 NIV)

4. The Lord instructs us to enjoy blessing the _____ he puts in our lives to serve.

> *You will be made rich in every way so that you can be generous on every occasion, and through us your generosity will result in thanksgiving to God.* (2 Corinthians 9:11 NIV)

Ultimately, the Lord wants us to use what he has given us for the benefit of others, especially the poor and needy. You do not need to give away all you possess to serve others, but God does want you to hold things loosely so you may lovingly minister to the people he puts in your life.

> *[17]Command those who are rich in this present world not to be arrogant nor to put their hope in wealth, which is so uncertain, but to put their hope in God, who richly provides us with everything for our enjoyment. [18]Command them to do good, to be rich in good deeds, and to be generous and willing to share. [19]In this way they will lay up treasure for themselves as a firm foundation for the coming age, so that they may take hold of the life that is truly life.* (1 Timothy 6:17–19 NIV)

ENJOY WHAT GOD HAS GIVEN YOU

Four Thieves of Joy

1. _____

²⁵"Therefore I tell you, do not worry about your life, what you will eat or drink; or about your body, what you will wear. Is not life more important than food, and the body more important than clothes? . . . ³³But seek first his kingdom and his righteousness, and all these things will be given to you as well. (Matthew 6:25, 33 NIV)

• **Replace your worry with** _____ **and** _____ .

Don't worry about anything; instead, pray about everything. Tell God what you need, and thank him for all he has done. (Philippians 4:6 NLT)

If I'm sleepless at midnight, I spend the hours in grateful reflection. (Psalm 63:6 MSG)

2. _____

When we compare ourselves to others there are only two possible outcomes. One is that we will think of ourselves as better than others, which is pride, or we will think of ourselves as worse than others, which is self-pity. Either outcome will rob you of your joy.

• **Replace comparison with** _____ .

¹²I know what it is to be in need, and I know what it is to have plenty. I have learned the secret of being content in any and every situation, whether well fed or hungry, whether living in plenty or in want. ¹³I can do everything through him who gives me strength. (Philippians 4:12–13 NIV)

But if we have food and clothing, we will be content with that. (1 Timothy 6:8 NIV)

Keep your lives free from the love of money and be content with what you have, because God has said, "Never will I leave you; never will I forsake you." (Hebrews 13:5 NIV)

3. _____

> *". . . first take the plank out of your own eye, and then you will see clearly to remove the speck from your brother's eye."* (Matthew 7:5 NIV)

- **Replace selfishness with** _____ .

> *. . . If you have money, share it generously . . .* (Romans 12:8 NLT)

> *"For even I, the Son of Man, came here not to be served but to serve others, and to give my life as a ransom for many."* (Mark 10:45 NLT)

4. _____

- **Replace false guilt with** _____ .

> *Therefore, there is now no condemnation for those who are in Christ Jesus.* (Romans 8:1 NIV)

> *[12]Wealth and honor come from you; you are the ruler of all things . . . [13]Now, our God, we give you thanks, and praise your glorious name.* (1 Chronicles 29:12–13 NIV)

> *Give thanks to the LORD, for he is good! His faithful love endures forever.* (Psalm 136:1 NLT)

Replacing these thieves is not a one-time choice! They are day-by-day and even moment-by-moment decisions. The thief comes to steal and destroy, but Christ came to give us true life and freedom (John 10:10).

Managing your finances God's way is just one part of managing your life God's way. And it all starts with surrendering your life to Jesus Christ.

We invite you to take the next ten minutes to watch the video feature by Rick Warren, *How to Become a Follower of Christ*. You will find this feature on your DVD or VHS tape.

ENJOY WHAT GOD HAS GIVEN YOU

DISCUSSION QUESTIONS .... 40 MINUTES

1. A few of you describe your initial reactions to the idea that God wants us to enjoy the resources he's given us. Does this statement surprise you? Why or why not?

2. Were you surprised to hear that God commands a Sabbath rest? What are we saying to the world around us when we obey God's commandment to rest from our labors?

3. What is the root of worry? How can it become a reminder to pray?

4. In our age of wall-to-wall advertising and 24/7 media, it's almost impossible not to get caught in the comparison game. How does it rob us of joy? What can we do to become free of it?

5. How does God ultimately want us to use what he has blessed us with? Discuss the idea of keeping a loose grip on things in our lives. How does that thinking change your world view?

LIVING ON PURPOSE .... 10 MINUTES

Worship

As we conclude this series, please make sure you've committed to put all the principles you've learned into practice. Remember that a full, abundant life of purpose can only be achieved free of financial entanglements. It's all about being available for God to do his work in and through your life while you're here on earth. This life is not about you. Managing your finances God's way is just part of a life fully surrendered to God. And a life fully surrendered to God is a life of worship.

As a group, read the following passage aloud. Consider committing it to memory as a help in reaching all your spiritual and financial goals.

> *¹Therefore, since we are surrounded by such a great a cloud of witnesses, let us throw off everything that hinders and the sin that so easily entangles, and let us run with perseverance the race marked out for us. ²Let us fix our eyes on Jesus, the author and perfecter of our faith, who for the joy set before him endured the cross, scorning its shame, and sat down at the right hand of the throne of God. ³Consider him who endured such opposition from sinful men, so that you will not grow weary and lose heart.* (Hebrews 12:1–3 NIV)

PRAYER DIRECTION .... 10 MINUTES

Take a few moments right now to express gratitude to God. Ask God to help you be faithful in pursuing financial freedom in your life.

FROM NOW ON . . .

Part of enjoying what God has given us is enjoying our relationships. Consider adding one more session to this study to focus on the purpose of fellowship. It's time to celebrate what God has done in your lives through this series. Take some time during that session to pray over each member of your group and commission one another for your life purpose.

Remember that managing money God's way is like every other aspect of the Christian life—it must be practiced daily and reviewed regularly. Discuss a plan with your spiritual partner to continue holding one another accountable for the action steps established throughout this study.

ENJOY WHAT GOD HAS GIVEN YOU

As a checklist of sorts, over the next week ask yourself the following questions:

• Have you grasped God's vision for your life?

• Are you faithfully using the financial tools introduced in this study?

• Have you recognized God's ownership of everything you have? Do you see your possessions as "on loan" from God? Consider a periodic renewing of your *Quit Claim Deed* as a reminder.

• How are you doing on your plan to allocate your own limited financial resources to the unlimited spending alternatives in your life? Are you spending less than you earn? Avoiding debt? Have you created an emergency fund? Do you have long term goals in mind, and on paper?

• What plan do you have for being generous with what God has entrusted to you? Have you begun to make this essential habit a regular part of your life?

• Have you established a saving and investing program?

- How is your debt repayment plan going? Are you beginning to make progress?

- Are you finding joy and contentment with what God has given you? God is glorified when we are grateful for what he has given us and truly enjoy what we have.

If you would like to study these issues in more depth, or if you have additional questions about financial management and planning, please visit www.crown.org.

We also invite you to visit our website at www.purposedriven.com where you will find many more video-based small group studies.

GROUP
DEVELOPMENT

SMALL GROUP RESOURCES

HELPS FOR HOSTS

Top Ten Ideas for New Hosts

Congratulations! As the host of your small group, you have responded to the call to help shepherd Jesus' flock. Few other tasks in the family of God surpass the contribution you will be making.

As you prepare to facilitate your group, whether it is one session or the entire series, here are a few additional thoughts to keep in mind. We encourage you to read and review these tips with each new discussion host before he or she leads.

Remember you are not alone. God knows everything about you, and he knew you would be asked to facilitate your group. Even though you may not feel ready, this is common for all good hosts. God promises, *"I will never leave you; I will never abandon you."* (Hebrews 13:5 TEV) Whether you are facilitating for one evening, several weeks, or a lifetime, you will be blessed as you serve.

1. **Don't try to do it alone.** Pray right now for God to help you build a healthy team. If you can enlist a co-host to help you shepherd the group, you will find your experience much richer. This is your chance to involve as many people as you can in building a healthy group. All you have to do is ask people to help. You'll be surprised at the response.

2. **Be friendly and be yourself.** God wants to use your unique gifts and temperament. Be sure to greet people at the door with a big smile . . . this can set the mood for the whole gathering. Remember, they are taking as big a step to show up at your house as you are to host this group! Don't try to do things exactly like another host; do them in a way that fits you. Admit when you don't have an answer and apologize when you make a mistake. Your group will love you for it and you'll sleep better at night.

3. **Prepare for your meeting ahead of time.** Review the video session before your group arrives. Write down your responses to each question. Pay special attention to exercises that ask group members to do something other than engage in discussion. These exercises will help your group live what the Bible teaches, not just talk about it. Be sure you understand how an exercise works. If the exercise employs one of the items in the Small Group Resources section (such as the Purpose Driven Group Guidelines), be sure to look over that item so you'll know how it works.

4. **Pray for your group members by name.** Before you begin your session, take a few moments and pray for each member by name. You may want to review the prayer list at least once a week. Ask God to use your time together to touch

the heart of every person in your group. Expect God to lead you to whomever he wants you to encourage or challenge in a special way. If you listen, God will surely lead.

5. **When you ask a question, be patient.** Someone will eventually respond. Sometimes people need a moment or two of silence to think about the question. If silence doesn't bother you, it won't bother anyone else. After someone responds, affirm the response with a simple "thanks" or "great answer." Then ask, "How about somebody else?" or "Would someone who hasn't shared like to add anything?" Be sensitive to new people or reluctant members who aren't ready to say, pray, or do anything. If you give them a safe setting, they will blossom over time. If someone in your group is a "wall flower" who sits silently through every session, consider talking to them privately and encouraging them to participate. Let them know how important they are to you—that they are loved and appreciated, and that the group would value their input. Remember, still water often runs deep.

6. **Provide transitions between questions.** Ask if anyone would like to read the paragraph or Bible passage. Don't call on anyone, but ask for a volunteer, and then be patient until someone begins. Be sure to thank the person who reads aloud.

7. **Break into smaller groups occasionally.** With a greater opportunity to talk in a small circle, people will connect more with the study, apply more quickly what they're learning, and ultimately get more out of their small group experience. A small circle also encourages a quiet person to participate and tends to minimize the effects of a more vocal or dominant member.

8. **Small circles are also helpful during prayer time.** People who are unaccustomed to praying aloud will feel more comfortable trying it with just two or three others. Also, prayer requests won't take as much time, so circles will have more time to actually pray. When you gather back with the whole group, you can have one person from each circle briefly update everyone on the prayer requests from their subgroups. The other great aspect of subgrouping is that it fosters leadership development. As you ask people in the group to facilitate discussion or to lead a prayer circle, it gives them a small leadership step that can build their confidence.

9. **Rotate facilitators occasionally.** You may be perfectly capable of hosting each time, but you will help others grow in their faith and gifts if you give them opportunities to host the group.

10. **One final challenge (for new or first-time hosts).** Before your first opportunity to lead, look up each of the six passages listed below. Read each one as a devotional exercise to help prepare you with a shepherd's heart. Trust us on this one. If you do this, you will be more than ready for your first meeting.

Matthew 9:36–38 (NIV)

[36] When Jesus saw the crowds, he had compassion on them, because they were harassed and helpless, like sheep without a shepherd. [37] Then he said to his disciples, "The harvest is plentiful but the workers are few. [38] Ask the Lord of the harvest, therefore, to send out workers into his harvest field."

John 10:14–15 (NIV)

[14] I am the good shepherd; I know my sheep and my sheep know me— [15] just as the Father knows me and I know the Father—and I lay down my life for the sheep.

1 Peter 5:2–4 (NIV)

[2] Be shepherds of God's flock that is under your care, serving as overseers—not because you must, but because you are willing, as God wants you to be; [3] not greedy for money, but eager to serve; not lording it over those entrusted to you, but being examples to the flock. [4] And when the Chief Shepherd appears, you will receive the crown of glory that will never fade away.

Philippians 2:1–5 (NIV)

[1] If you have any encouragement from being united with Christ, if any comfort from his love, if any fellowship with the Spirit, if any tenderness and compassion, [2] then make my joy complete by being like-minded, having the same love, being one in spirit and purpose. [3] Do nothing out of selfish ambition or vain conceit, but in humility consider others better than yourselves. [4] Each of you should look not only to your own interests, but also to the interests of others. [5] Your attitude should be the same as that of Jesus Christ.

Hebrews 10:23–25 (NIV)

[23] Let us hold unswervingly to the hope we profess, for he who promised is faithful. [24] And let us consider how we may spur one another on toward love and good deeds. [25] Let us not give up meeting together, as some are in the habit of doing, but let us encourage one another—and all the more as you see the Day approaching.

1 Thessalonians 2:7–8, 11–12 (NIV)

[7] . . . but we were gentle among you, like a mother caring for her little children. [8] We loved you so much that we were delighted to share with you not only the Gospel of God but our lives as well, because you had become so dear to us. . . . [11] For you know that we dealt with each of you as a father deals with his own children, [12] encouraging, comforting and urging you to live lives worthy of God, who calls you into his kingdom and glory.

FREQUENTLY ASKED QUESTIONS

How long will this group meet?

Managing Our Finances God's Way is seven weeks long. We encourage your group to add an eighth week for a celebration. In your final session, each group member may decide if he or she desires to continue on for another study. At that time you may also want to do some informal evaluation, discuss your Group Guidelines, and decide which study you want to do next. We recommend you visit our website at www.purposedriven.com for more video-based small group studies.

Who is the host?

The host is the person who coordinates and facilitates your group meetings. In addition to a host, we encourage you to select one or more group members to lead your group discussions. Several other responsibilities can be rotated, including refreshments, prayer requests, worship, or keeping up with those who miss a meeting. Shared ownership in the group helps everybody grow.

Where do we find new group members?

Recruiting new members can be a challenge for groups, especially new groups with just a few people, or existing groups that lose a few people along the way. We encourage you to use the *Circles of Life* diagram on page 105 of this workbook to brainstorm a list of people from your workplace, church, school, neighborhood, family, and so on. Then pray for the people on each member's list. Allow each member to invite several people from their list. Some groups fear that newcomers will interrupt the intimacy that members have built over time. However, groups that welcome newcomers generally gain strength with the infusion of new blood. Remember, the next person you add just might become a friend for eternity. Logistically, groups find different ways to add members. Some groups remain permanently open, while others choose to open periodically, such as at the beginning or end of a study. If your group becomes too large for easy, face-to-face conversations, you can subgroup, forming a second discussion group in another room.

How do we handle the childcare needs in our group?

Childcare needs must be handled very carefully. This is a sensitive issue. We suggest you seek creative solutions as a group. One common solution is to have the adults meet in the living room and share the cost of a baby sitter (or two) who can be with the kids in another part of the house. Another popular option is to have one home for the kids and a second home (close by) for the adults. If desired, the adults could rotate the responsibility of providing a lesson for the kids. This last option is great with school age kids and can be a huge blessing to families.

PURPOSE DRIVEN GROUP GUIDELINES

It's a good idea for every group to put words to their shared values, expectations, and commitments. Such guidelines will help you avoid unspoken agendas and unmet expectations. We recommend you discuss your guidelines during the *Introduction* session in order to lay the foundation for a healthy group experience. Feel free to modify anything that does not work for your group.

We agree to the following values:

Clear Purpose	To grow healthy spiritual lives by building a healthy small group community
Group Attendance	To give priority to the group meeting (call if I am absent or late)
Safe Environment	To create a safe place where people can be heard and feel loved (no quick answers, snap judgments, or simple fixes)
Be Confidential	To keep anything that is shared strictly confidential and within the group
Conflict Resolution	To avoid gossip and to immediately resolve any concerns by following the principles of Matthew 18:15–17
Spiritual Health	To give group members permission to speak into my life and help me live a healthy, balanced spiritual life that is pleasing to God
Limit Our Freedom	To limit our freedom by not serving or consuming alcohol during small group meetings or events so as to avoid causing a weaker brother or sister to stumble (1 Corinthians 8:1–13; Romans 14:19–21)
Welcome Newcomers	To invite friends who might benefit from this study and warmly welcome newcomers
Building Relationships	To get to know the other members of the group and pray for them regularly
Other	_____
	_____

We have also discussed and agree on the following items:

Child Care	_____
Starting Time	_____
Ending Time	_____

If you haven't already done so, take a few minutes to fill out the Small Group Calendar on page 108.

CIRCLES OF LIFE — SMALL GROUP CONNECTIONS

Discover who you can connect in community

Use this chart to help carry out one of the values in the Group Guidelines, to "Welcome Newcomers."

"Follow me, and I will make you fishers of men."
Matthew 4:19 (KJV)

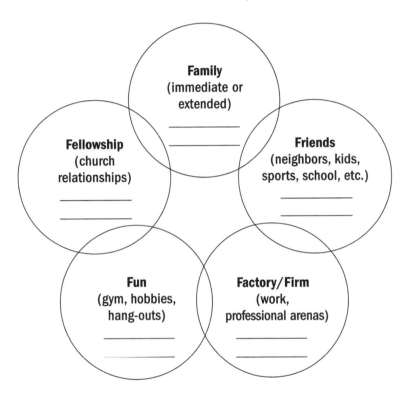

Follow this simple three-step process:

1. List one to two people in each circle.

2. Prayerfully select one person or couple from your list and tell your group about them.

3. Give them a call and invite them to your next meeting. Over fifty percent of those invited to a small group say, "Yes!"

SMALL GROUP PRAYER AND PRAISE REPORT

This is a place where you can write each other's requests for prayer. You can also make a note when God answers a prayer. Pray for each other's requests. If you're new to group prayer, it's okay to pray silently or to pray by using just one sentence:

"God, please help _____ to _____ ."

DATE	PERSON	PRAYER REQUEST	PRAISE REPORT

DATE	PERSON	PRAYER REQUEST	PRAISE REPORT

SMALL GROUP CALENDAR

Healthy groups share responsibilities and group ownership. It might take some time for this to develop. Shared ownership ensures that responsibility for the group doesn't fall to one person. Use the calendar to keep track of social events, mission projects, birthdays, or days off. Complete this calendar at your first or second meeting. Planning ahead will increase attendance and shared ownership.

DATE	LESSON	LOCATION	FACILITATOR	SNACK OR MEAL
10/22	Session 2	Steve & Laura	Bill Jones	John & Alice

ANSWER KEY

Introduction — The Big Picture:

- In Christ's kingdom, we understand that the purpose for earthly wealth is to invest it in **eternal treasures**.

- God desires to work through ordinary **people** with ordinary **finances**.

God wants to do something of eternal **significance** through your life.

First misconception: Money is **evil**.

Second misconception: Money is the **key to happiness**.

- Financial freedom is not determined by how much money you make. It's determined by how you **spend what you have**.

- In other words, most of us don't have a **money** problem. We have a **management** problem.

- Without self-control, our **yearning** capacity will always exceed our **earning** capacity.

A truly wealthy person is a person who is **content** with what he or she has.

Session One — Dedicate It All to God:

God **owns** everything.

You are his **money manager**.

- **Time**
- **Spouses**
- **Children**
- **Money**
- **Spiritual gifts**
- **The Gospel**
- **People**

1. It all belongs to **him**.

2. You are his **money manager**.

3. You cannot serve **two masters**.

4. You can make an impact on **eternity**.

5. God blesses that which we **dedicate** to him.

Session Two — Plan Your Spending:

1. Spend less than you **earn**.

2. Avoid the use of **debt**.

3. Build an **emergency** fund.

4. Set **long-term** goals.

Giving is a **first priority**.

A **little** bit over a **long** time frame makes a **big** difference.

If I borrow money, I am **obligated** to repay it.

a) **Provide** for my family.

b) Have a lifestyle I am **content** with.

c) **Enjoy** what God has given me.

- There is no such thing as an **independent** financial decision.

- The longer the perspective, the better the financial **decisions**.

- Financial **maturity**: Giving up today's desires for future benefits.

1. Pray together for God's **guidance**.

2. Look **honestly** at where you are.

3. **Prioritize** your needs and goals.

4. Prepare a **workable** plan.

5. Practice keeping good **records**.

Session Three — Giving As an Act of Worship:

1. God **blesses** generous people

   • Emotional **happiness**

   • Spiritual **holiness**

   • Material **prosperity**

2. God provides a **pathway** for generous people

   a. Biblical generosity give the **first** and the **best** to God.

      • The first tenth belongs to God. It's called a **tithe**.

   b. Biblical generosity is **regular** and **systematic**.

   c. Biblical generosity is **proportional** to our income.

   d. Biblical generosity involves **sacrifice**.

   e. Biblical generosity is thoughtful, voluntary, and **worshipful**.

3 Generosity begins with a **step of faith**.

Session Four — Saving and Investing:

• Wealth is typically **created** by a career or vocation over a long time frame.

• Wealth is **preserved** by a diversified investment strategy.

Step 1: Pay off **credit card** debt.

Step 2: Set money aside for an **emergency fund**.

Step 3: Save for **major purchases**.

Step 4: Diversify your investments to meet **long-term needs**.

Step 5: Begin taking calculated financial **risks**.

Look for **godly counsel** to make your investment decisions.

Session Five — God's Solution to Debt:

1. **Pray**.

2. Develop a **debt-free** mind set.

3. List **all your debts**.

4. List everything **you own**.

5. Establish a **spending plan**.

6. Establish a **repayment** schedule.

7. Consider earning **additional income**.

8. Consider a radical change in your **lifestyle**.

9. Don't **give up**!

Session Six — Enjoy What God Has Given You:

We are God's **managers**.

God truly wants us to **enjoy** the resources that he has given us.

1. The Lord expects us to take care of **our families**.

2. The Lord wants us to enjoy regular periods of **rest and refreshment**.

3. The Lord tells us that when we enjoy his blessings, we bring him more **glory**.

4. The Lord instructs us to enjoy blessing the **people** he puts in our lives to serve.

Four Thieves of Joy:

1. **Worry**

   • Replace your worry with **trust** and **prayer**.

2. **Comparison**

   • Replace comparison with **contentment**.

3. **Selfishness**

   • Replace selfishness with **sacrifice**.

4. **False guilt**

   • Replace false guilt with **gratitude**.

KEY VERSES

One of the most effective ways to drive deeply into our lives the principles we are learning in this series is to internalize key Scriptures. We encourage you to stretch yourself and meditate, memorize, or reflect on these verses. Read the "Key Verse" each week together as a group.

*I have hidden your word in my heart that
I might not sin against you.*

Psalm 119:11 (NIV)

Introduction

Tell them to use their money to do good . . . by doing this they will be storing up real treasure for themselves in heaven—it is the only safe investment for eternity!

1 Timothy 6:18a-19a (LB)

Session 1

Everything in the heavens and on earth is yours, O Lord, and this is your kingdom. We adore you as the one who is over all things. Riches and honor come from you alone, for you rule over everything. Power and might are in your hand, and it is at your discretion that people are made great and given strength.

1 Chronicles 29:11b-12 (NLT)

Session 2

Good planning and hard work lead to prosperity, but hasty shortcuts lead to poverty.

Proverbs 21:5 (NLT)

Session 3

You should remember the words of the Lord Jesus: "It is more blessed to give than to receive."

Acts 20:35b (NLT)

Session 4

The servant to whom he had entrusted the five bags of gold said, "Sir, you gave me five bags of gold to invest, and I have doubled the amount." The master was full of praise. "Well done, my good and faithful servant. You have been faithful in handling this small amount, so now I will give you many more responsibilities. Let's celebrate together!"

Matthew 25:20-21 (NLT)

Session 5

Let no debt remain outstanding, except the continuing debt to love one another, for he who loves his fellowman has fulfilled the law.

Romans 13:8 (NIV)

Session 6

When God gives any man wealth and possessions, and enables him to enjoy them, to accept his lot and be happy in his work—this is a gift of God.

Ecclesiastes 5:19 (NIV)

Quit Claim Card

On this day, I hereby acknowledge that God owns all of my earthly possessions. I am simply his steward.

Thank you, Lord. Help me to be a wise and faithful manager of the resources you have put in my hands. Amen.

Name _____ Date _____

NOTES

APPENDIX

FORMS AND WORKSHEETS

MANAGING FINANCES GOD'S WAY – PRACTICAL APPLICATION WORKSHEET

PurposeDriven®

TRANSACTION RECORD

CROWN FINANCIAL MINISTRIES

(If you desire to have a transaction/check register for your spending categories, please use this worksheet.)

Date	Check #	Transaction	Spending Category	Deposit	Withdrawal
				$	$
				$	$
				$	$
				$	$
				$	$
				$	$
				$	$
				$	$
				$	$
				$	$
				$	$
				$	$
				$	$
				$	$
				$	$
				$	$
				$	$
				$	$
				$	$
				$	$
				$	$
				$	$
				$	$
				$	$
				$	$
				$	$
				$	$
				$	$
				$	$
				$	$
				$	$
				$	$
				$	$
				$	$
				$	$
				$	$
				$	$
				$	$
				$	$
				$	$
				$	$
				$	$
				$	$
				$	$
				$	$
				$	$
				$	$
				$	$

))) PurposeDriven®

TRANSACTION RECORD

CROWN FINANCIAL MINISTRIES

(If you desire to have a transaction/check register for your spending categories, please use this worksheet.)

Date	Check #	Transaction	Spending Category	Deposit	Withdrawal
				$	$
				$	$
				$	$
				$	$
				$	$
				$	$
				$	$
				$	$
				$	$
				$	$
				$	$
				$	$
				$	$
				$	$
				$	$
				$	$
				$	$
				$	$
				$	$
				$	$
				$	$
				$	$
				$	$
				$	$
				$	$
				$	$
				$	$
				$	$
				$	$
				$	$
				$	$
				$	$
				$	$
				$	$
				$	$
				$	$
				$	$
				$	$
				$	$
				$	$
				$	$
				$	$
				$	$
				$	$
				$	$
				$	$
				$	$

MANAGING FINANCES GOD'S WAY – PRACTICAL APPLICATION WORKSHEET

PurposeDriven®

TRANSACTION RECORD

CROWN FINANCIAL MINISTRIES

(If you desire to have a transaction/check register for your spending categories, please use this worksheet.)

Date	Check #	Transaction	Spending Category	Deposit	Withdrawal
				$	$
				$	$
				$	$
				$	$
				$	$
				$	$
				$	$
				$	$
				$	$
				$	$
				$	$
				$	$
				$	$
				$	$
				$	$
				$	$
				$	$
				$	$
				$	$
				$	$
				$	$
				$	$
				$	$
				$	$
				$	$
				$	$
				$	$
				$	$
				$	$
				$	$
				$	$
				$	$
				$	$
				$	$
				$	$
				$	$
				$	$
				$	$
				$	$
				$	$
				$	$
				$	$
				$	$
				$	$
				$	$
				$	$
				$	$
				$	$
				$	$
				$	$
				$	$
				$	$
				$	$

))) PurposeDriven®

TRANSACTION RECORD

CROWN FINANCIAL MINISTRIES

(If you desire to have a transaction/check register for your spending categories, please use this worksheet.)

Date	Check #	Transaction	Spending Category	Deposit	Withdrawal
				$	$
				$	$
				$	$
				$	$
				$	$
				$	$
				$	$
				$	$
				$	$
				$	$
				$	$
				$	$
				$	$
				$	$
				$	$
				$	$
				$	$
				$	$
				$	$
				$	$
				$	$
				$	$
				$	$
				$	$
				$	$
				$	$
				$	$
				$	$
				$	$
				$	$
				$	$
				$	$
				$	$
				$	$
				$	$
				$	$
				$	$
				$	$
				$	$
				$	$
				$	$
				$	$
				$	$
				$	$
				$	$
				$	$
				$	$
				$	$
				$	$

》PurposeDriven®

PERSONAL FINANCIAL PROFILE

CROWN FINANCIAL MINISTRIES

Name:

Date:

WHAT I OWN (Assets)
(Please fill in all sections as well as you can)

CATEGORY	CURRENT VALUES	
Checking Accounts	$	
Savings Accounts	$	
Money Market Accounts	$	
Certificates of Deposit	$	
Stocks / Bonds / Mutual Funds	$	
Life Insurance (Cash Value)	$	
Primary Residence (Market Value)	$	
Other Real Estate	$	
Car #1 Resale Value	$	
Car #2 Resale Value	$	
Car #3 Resale Value	$	
Other Personal Property	$	
IRAs / Retirement Funds / 401K	$	
Other (i.e., Business . . .)	$	
	TOTAL ASSETS:	$

WHAT I OWE (Liabilities)
(Please fill in all sections as well as you can)

CATEGORY	DEBT NAME	MONTHLY PAYMENT	INTEREST %	TOTAL BALANCE
Mortgage / Rent		$	%	$
Additional Real Estate Loan		$	%	$
Car #1 Payment		$	%	$
Car #2 Payment		$	%	$
Car #3 Payment		$	%	$
		$	%	$
		$	%	$
Mortgage and Car Debt Subtotal:		$		$
Credit Cards		$	%	$
		$	%	$
		$	%	$
		$	%	$
		$	%	$
		$	%	$
		$	%	$
		$	%	$
Other Debts (personal loans, student loans, business debt, medical, legal, IRS, etc.)		$	%	$
		$	%	$
		$	%	$
		$	%	$
		$	%	$
		$	%	$
Credit Cards and Other Subtotals:		$		$
	TOTAL MONTHLY PAYMENTS:	$	**TOTAL DEBT:**	$
	TOTAL ASSETS – TOTAL DEBT =		**NET WORTH:**	$

Quit Claim Deed

This Quit Claim Deed, Made the _____ day of _____

From: _____

To: The Lord

I (we) hereby transfer to the Lord the ownership of the following possessions:

_____

_____

_____

_____

_____

_____

_____

_____

_____

_____

Stewards of the possessions above:

_____

_____

Witnesses who hold me (us) accountable
in the recognition of the Lord's ownership:

_____

_____

_____

_____

This instrument is not a binding legal document and cannot be used to transfer property.

PurposeDriven®

MONTHLY INCOME & PRIORITY EXPENSES

CROWN FINANCIAL MINISTRIES

(Add totals on this page to the "Spending Plan" page)

Name:

Date:

Monthly Income			
Monthly Salary #1	$		
Monthly Salary #2	$		
Interest Income	$		
Dividends	$		
Commissions	$		
Bonuses / Tips	$		
Retirement Income #1	$		
Retirement Income #2	$		
Net Business Income	$		
Other Income	$		
GROSS MONTHLY INCOME	Amount	$	

Priority Expenses			
The Local Church	$		
The Poor	$		
Other Ministries	$		
Other Giving	$		
Tithing/Giving (Monthly)	Amount	$	

Federal	$		
Medicare	$		
Social Security (FICA)	$		
State	$		
Local	$		
Other	$		
Other	$		
Taxes (Monthly)	Amount	$	

Savings Account #1	$		
Savings Account #2	$		
Credit Union #1	$		
Credit Union #2	$		
Other	$		
Savings (Monthly)	Amount	$	

401K / 403b Plans	$		
College Funds	$		
Stock, Bonds, Mutual Funds	$		
Real Estate	$		
Other	$		
Investments (Monthly)	Amount	$	

$

MANAGING FINANCES GOD'S WAY – PRACTICAL APPLICATION WORKSHEET

))) PurposeDriven®

SPENDING PLAN

CROWN FINANCIAL MINISTRIES

Name:

Date:

For annual expenses, please divide by twelve and enter a monthly amount.

From Income & Priority Expense pages

GROSS MONTHLY INCOME	$
TITHING / GIVING	$
TAXES	$
SAVINGS	$
INVESTMENTS	$
DEBT REPAYMENT (from Personal Financial Statement)	$
NET SPENDABLE INCOME	$

HOUSING

Mortgage / Rent	$
Taxes	$
Home Insurance	$
Association Dues	$
Additional Real Estate Loan	$
Home Maintenance	$
Electrical	$
Gas	$
Water	$
Garbage	$
Telephone	$
Cell Phone	$
Furnishings	$
Internet Service	$
Other	$
Other	$
TOTAL	$

TRANSPORTATION

Car Payment	$
Car Payment	$
Car Payment	$
Auto Insurance	$
License / Registration	$
Gas and Oil	$
Auto Maintenance	$
Auto Replacement Fund	$
Other (tolls/parking/transit fares)	$
Other	$
TOTAL	$

INSURANCE

Life Insurance	$
Health Insurance	$
Dental Insurance	$
Disability Insurance	$
Other	$
TOTAL	$

HOUSEHOLD / PERSONAL

Food / Groceries / Toiletries	$
Beauty / Barber	$
Laundry / Dry Cleaning	$
Books / Subscriptions	$
Gifts	$
Clothing (Adult and Children)	$
Education / Tuition / School Supplies	$
Lessons / Tutoring	$
Allowance	$
Child Support	$
Other	$
TOTAL	$

MEDICAL / FAMILY / PROFESSIONAL

Child Care	
Medical / Dental / Vision	
Prescription / Glasses / Contacts	
Legal	
Counseling	
Profession Dues / Memberships	
Other	
Other	
Other	
TOTAL	$

ENTERTAINMENT / RECREATION

Dining Out	
Lunch / Snacks	
Movies / Events	
Baby-sitting	
Vacation / Trips	
Cable TV	
Books / Subscriptions	
Health Club / Hobbies	
Pets	
Cash	
Other	
TOTAL	$

TOTAL EXPENSES	$
NET SPENDABLE INCOME (from 1st column above)	$
VARIANCE	$

MANAGING FINANCES GOD'S WAY – PRACTICAL APPLICATION WORKSHEET

PurposeDriven®

SPENDING PLAN

CROWN FINANCIAL MINISTRIES

Name:

Date:

For annual expenses, please divide by twelve and enter a monthly amount.

From Income & Priority Expense pages

GROSS MONTHLY INCOME	$
TITHING / GIVING	$
TAXES	$
SAVINGS	$
INVESTMENTS	$
DEBT REPAYMENT (from Personal Financial Statement)	$
NET SPENDABLE INCOME	$

HOUSING

Mortgage / Rent	$
Taxes	$
Home Insurance	$
Association Dues	$
Additional Real Estate Loan	$
Home Maintenance	$
Electrical	$
Gas	$
Water	$
Garbage	$
Telephone	$
Cell Phone	$
Furnishings	$
Internet Service	$
Other	$
Other	$
TOTAL	$

TRANSPORTATION

Car Payment	$
Car Payment	$
Car Payment	$
Auto Insurance	$
License / Registration	$
Gas and Oil	$
Auto Maintenance	$
Auto Replacement Fund	$
Other (tolls/parking/transit fares)	$
Other	$
TOTAL	$

INSURANCE

Life Insurance	$
Health Insurance	$
Dental Insurance	$
Disability Insurance	$
Other	$
TOTAL	$

HOUSEHOLD / PERSONAL

Food / Groceries / Toiletries	$
Beauty / Barber	$
Laundry / Dry Cleaning	$
Books / Subscriptions	$
Gifts	$
Clothing (Adult and Children)	$
Education / Tuition / School Supplies	$
Lessons / Tutoring	$
Allowance	$
Child Support	$
Other	$
TOTAL	$

MEDICAL / FAMILY / PROFESSIONAL

Child Care	
Medical / Dental / Vision	
Prescription / Glasses / Contacts	
Legal	
Counseling	
Profession Dues / Memberships	
Other	
Other	
Other	
TOTAL	$

ENTERTAINMENT / RECREATION

Dining Out	
Lunch / Snacks	
Movies / Events	
Baby-sitting	
Vacation / Trips	
Cable TV	
Books / Subscriptions	
Health Club / Hobbies	
Pets	
Cash	
Other	
TOTAL	$

TOTAL EXPENSES	$
NET SPENDABLE INCOME (from 1st column above)	$
VARIANCE	$

MANAGING FINANCES GOD'S WAY – PRACTICAL APPLICATION WORKSHEET

PurposeDriven®

MONTHLY EXPENSES

CROWN FINANCIAL MINISTRIES

Month: _____ **Year:** _____

Category	GROSS INCOME	TITHE/GIVING	TAXES	Savings	Investments	Debt Repayment	Housing
PLANNED AMOUNT	$	$	$	$	$	$	$
Date							
1							
2							
3							
4							
5							
6							
7							
8							
9							
10							
11							
12							
13							
14							
15							
This month SUBTOTAL	$	$	$	$	$	$	$
16							
17							
18							
19							
20							
21							
22							
23							
24							
25							
26							
27							
28							
29							
30							
31							
This month ACTUAL	$	$	$	$	$	$	$
This month vs. PLAN	$	$	$	$	$	$	$
Year to Date PLAN	$	$	$	$	$	$	$
Year to Date ACTUAL	$	$	$	$	$	$	$
Year to Date ACTUAL vs. PLAN	$	$	$	$	$	$	$

SPENDING SUMMARY

This Month		Previous Month / Year to Date		Year to Date
Total Gross Income $_____		Total Gross Income $_____		Total Gross Income $_____
Minus Total Expenses $_____	**+**	Minus Total Expenses $_____	**=**	Minus Total Expenses $_____
Equals Surplus/Deficit $_____		Equals Surplus/Deficit $_____		Equals Surplus/Deficit $_____

PurposeDriven®

MONTHLY EXPENSES

CROWN FINANCIAL MINISTRIES

Category	Transportation	Insurance	Household/ Personal	Medical/Family/ Professional	Entertainment/ Recreation	TOTAL EXPENSES	This Month SURPLUS/ DEFICIT
PLANNED AMOUNT	$	$	$	$	$	$	$
Date							
1						$	$
2						$	$
3						$	$
4						$	$
5						$	$
6						$	$
7						$	$
8						$	$
9						$	$
10						$	$
11						$	$
12						$	$
13						$	$
14						$	$
15						$	$
This month SUBTOTAL	$	$	$	$	$	$	$
16						$	$
17						$	$
18						$	$
19						$	$
20						$	$
21						$	$
22						$	$
23						$	$
24						$	$
25						$	$
26						$	$
27						$	$
28						$	$
29						$	$
30						$	$
31						$	$
This month ACTUAL	$	$	$	$	$	$	$
This month vs. PLAN	$	$	$	$	$	$	$
Year to Date PLAN	$	$	$	$	$	$	$
Year to Date ACTUAL	$	$	$	$	$	$	$
Year to Date ACTUAL vs. PLAN	$	$	$	$	$	$	$

MANAGING FINANCES GOD'S WAY – PRACTICAL APPLICATION WORKSHEET

PurposeDriven®

MONTHLY EXPENSES

CROWN FINANCIAL MINISTRIES

Month: _____ **Year:** _____

Category	GROSS INCOME	TITHE/GIVING	TAXES	Savings	Investments	Debt Repayment	Housing
PLANNED AMOUNT	$	$	$	$	$	$	$
Date							
1							
2							
3							
4							
5							
6							
7							
8							
9							
10							
11							
12							
13							
14							
15							
This month SUBTOTAL	$	$	$	$	$	$	$
16							
17							
18							
19							
20							
21							
22							
23							
24							
25							
26							
27							
28							
29							
30							
31							
This month ACTUAL	$	$	$	$	$	$	$
This month vs. PLAN	$	$	$	$	$	$	$
Year to Date PLAN	$	$	$	$	$	$	$
Year to Date ACTUAL	$	$	$	$	$	$	$
Year to Date ACTUAL vs. PLAN	$	$	$	$	$	$	$

SPENDING SUMMARY

This Month		Previous Month / Year to Date		Year to Date
Total Gross Income $_____		Total Gross Income $_____		Total Gross Income $_____
Minus Total Expenses $_____	**+**	Minus Total Expenses $_____	**=**	Minus Total Expenses $_____
Equals Surplus/Deficit $_____		Equals Surplus/Deficit $_____		Equals Surplus/Deficit $_____

PurposeDriven®

MONTHLY EXPENSES

CROWN FINANCIAL MINISTRIES

Category	Transportation	Insurance	Household/ Personal	Medical/Family/ Professional	Entertainment/ Recreation	TOTAL EXPENSES	This Month SURPLUS/ DEFICIT
PLANNED AMOUNT	$	$	$	$	$	$	$
Date							
1						$	$
2						$	$
3						$	$
4						$	$
5						$	$
6						$	$
7						$	$
8						$	$
9						$	$
10						$	$
11						$	$
12						$	$
13						$	$
14						$	$
15						$	$
This month SUBTOTAL	$	$	$	$	$	$	$
16						$	$
17						$	$
18						$	$
19						$	$
20						$	$
21						$	$
22						$	$
23						$	$
24						$	$
25						$	$
26						$	$
27						$	$
28						$	$
29						$	$
30						$	$
31						$	$
This month ACTUAL	$	$	$	$	$	$	$
This month vs. PLAN	$	$	$	$	$	$	$
Year to Date PLAN	$	$	$	$	$	$	$
Year to Date ACTUAL	$	$	$	$	$	$	$
Year to Date ACTUAL vs. PLAN	$	$	$	$	$	$	$

MANAGING FINANCES GOD'S WAY – PRACTICAL APPLICATION WORKSHEET

PurposeDriven®

MONTHLY EXPENSES

CROWN FINANCIAL MINISTRIES

Month: _____ **Year:** _____

Category	GROSS INCOME	TITHE/GIVING	TAXES	Savings	Investments	Debt Repayment	Housing
PLANNED AMOUNT	$	$	$	$	$	$	$
Date							
1							
2							
3							
4							
5							
6							
7							
8							
9							
10							
11							
12							
13							
14							
15							
This month SUBTOTAL	$	$	$	$	$	$	$
16							
17							
18							
19							
20							
21							
22							
23							
24							
25							
26							
27							
28							
29							
30							
31							
This month ACTUAL	$	$	$	$	$	$	$
This month vs. PLAN	$	$	$	$	$	$	$
Year to Date PLAN	$	$	$	$	$	$	$
Year to Date ACTUAL	$	$	$	$	$	$	$
Year to Date ACTUAL vs. PLAN	$	$	$	$	$	$	$

SPENDING SUMMARY

This Month		Previous Month / Year to Date		Year to Date
Total Gross Income $_____		Total Gross Income $_____		Total Gross Income $_____
Minus Total Expenses $_____	**+**	Minus Total Expenses $_____	**=**	Minus Total Expenses $_____
Equals Surplus/Deficit $_____		Equals Surplus/Deficit $_____		Equals Surplus/Deficit $_____

PurposeDriven®   **MONTHLY EXPENSES**   CROWN FINANCIAL MINISTRIES

Category	Transportation	Insurance	Household/ Personal	Medical/Family/ Professional	Entertainment/ Recreation	TOTAL EXPENSES	This Month SURPLUS/ DEFICIT
PLANNED AMOUNT	$	$	$	$	$	$	$
Date							
1						$	$
2						$	$
3						$	$
4						$	$
5						$	$
6						$	$
7						$	$
8						$	$
9						$	$
10						$	$
11						$	$
12						$	$
13						$	$
14						$	$
15						$	$
This month SUBTOTAL	$	$	$	$	$	$	$
16						$	$
17						$	$
18						$	$
19						$	$
20						$	$
21						$	$
22						$	$
23						$	$
24						$	$
25						$	$
26						$	$
27						$	$
28						$	$
29						$	$
30						$	$
31						$	$
This month ACTUAL	$	$	$	$	$	$	$
This month vs. PLAN	$	$	$	$	$	$	$
Year to Date PLAN	$	$	$	$	$	$	$
Year to Date ACTUAL	$	$	$	$	$	$	$
Year to Date ACTUAL vs. PLAN	$	$	$	$	$	$	$

PurposeDriven®

MONTHLY EXPENSES

CROWN FINANCIAL MINISTRIES

Month: [   ] **Year:** [   ]

Category	GROSS INCOME	TITHE/GIVING	TAXES	Savings	Investments	Debt Repayment	Housing
PLANNED AMOUNT	$	$	$	$	$	$	$
Date							
1							
2							
3							
4							
5							
6							
7							
8							
9							
10							
11							
12							
13							
14							
15							
This month SUBTOTAL	$	$	$	$	$	$	$
16							
17							
18							
19							
20							
21							
22							
23							
24							
25							
26							
27							
28							
29							
30							
31							
This month ACTUAL	$	$	$	$	$	$	$
This month vs. PLAN	$	$	$	$	$	$	$
Year to Date PLAN	$	$	$	$	$	$	$
Year to Date ACTUAL	$	$	$	$	$	$	$
Year to Date ACTUAL vs. PLAN	$	$	$	$	$	$	$

SPENDING SUMMARY

This Month		**Previous Month / Year to Date**		**Year to Date**
Total Gross Income $_____		Total Gross Income $_____		Total Gross Income $_____
Minus Total Expenses $_____	**+**	Minus Total Expenses $_____	**=**	Minus Total Expenses $_____
Equals Surplus/Deficit $_____		Equals Surplus/Deficit $_____		Equals Surplus/Deficit $_____

>))PurposeDriven®

MONTHLY EXPENSES

CROWN FINANCIAL MINISTRIES

Category	Transportation	Insurance	Household/ Personal	Medical/Family/ Professional	Entertainment/ Recreation	TOTAL EXPENSES	This Month SURPLUS/ DEFICIT
PLANNED AMOUNT	$	$	$	$	$	$	$
Date							
1						$	$
2						$	$
3						$	$
4						$	$
5						$	$
6						$	$
7						$	$
8						$	$
9						$	$
10						$	$
11						$	$
12						$	$
13						$	$
14						$	$
15						$	$
This month SUBTOTAL	$	$	$	$	$	$	$
16						$	$
17						$	$
18						$	$
19						$	$
20						$	$
21						$	$
22						$	$
23						$	$
24						$	$
25						$	$
26						$	$
27						$	$
28						$	$
29						$	$
30						$	$
31						$	$
This month ACTUAL	$	$	$	$	$	$	$
This month vs. PLAN	$	$	$	$	$	$	$
Year to Date PLAN	$	$	$	$	$	$	$
Year to Date ACTUAL	$	$	$	$	$	$	$
Year to Date ACTUAL vs. PLAN	$	$	$	$	$	$	$

PurposeDriven®

MONTHLY EXPENSES

CROWN FINANCIAL MINISTRIES

Month: [   ]   **Year:** [   ]

Category	GROSS INCOME	TITHE/GIVING	TAXES	Savings	Investments	Debt Repayment	Housing
PLANNED AMOUNT	$	$	$	$	$	$	$
Date							
1							
2							
3							
4							
5							
6							
7							
8							
9							
10							
11							
12							
13							
14							
15							
This month SUBTOTAL	$	$	$	$	$	$	$
16							
17							
18							
19							
20							
21							
22							
23							
24							
25							
26							
27							
28							
29							
30							
31							
This month ACTUAL	$	$	$	$	$	$	$
This month vs. PLAN	$	$	$	$	$	$	$
Year to Date PLAN	$	$	$	$	$	$	$
Year to Date ACTUAL	$	$	$	$	$	$	$
Year to Date ACTUAL vs. PLAN	$	$	$	$	$	$	$

SPENDING SUMMARY

This Month		Previous Month / Year to Date		Year to Date
Total Gross Income $_____		Total Gross Income $_____		Total Gross Income $_____
Minus Total Expenses $_____	**+**	Minus Total Expenses $_____	**=**	Minus Total Expenses $_____
Equals Surplus/Deficit $_____		Equals Surplus/Deficit $_____		Equals Surplus/Deficit $_____

PurposeDriven®

MONTHLY EXPENSES

CROWN FINANCIAL MINISTRIES

Category	Transportation	Insurance	Household/ Personal	Medical/Family/ Professional	Entertainment/ Recreation	TOTAL EXPENSES	This Month SURPLUS/ DEFICIT
PLANNED AMOUNT	$	$	$	$	$	$	$
Date							
1						$	$
2						$	$
3						$	$
4						$	$
5						$	$
6						$	$
7						$	$
8						$	$
9						$	$
10						$	$
11						$	$
12						$	$
13						$	$
14						$	$
15						$	$
This month SUBTOTAL	$	$	$	$	$	$	$
16						$	$
17						$	$
18						$	$
19						$	$
20						$	$
21						$	$
22						$	$
23						$	$
24						$	$
25						$	$
26						$	$
27						$	$
28						$	$
29						$	$
30						$	$
31						$	$
This month ACTUAL	$	$	$	$	$	$	$
This month vs. PLAN	$	$	$	$	$	$	$
Year to Date PLAN	$	$	$	$	$	$	$
Year to Date ACTUAL	$	$	$	$	$	$	$
Year to Date ACTUAL vs. PLAN	$	$	$	$	$	$	$

MANAGING FINANCES GOD'S WAY – PRACTICAL APPLICATION WORKSHEET

)))PurposeDriven®

MONTHLY EXPENSES

CROWN FINANCIAL MINISTRIES

Month: [ ] **Year:** [ ]

Category	GROSS INCOME	TITHE/GIVING	TAXES	Savings	Investments	Debt Repayment	Housing
PLANNED AMOUNT	$	$	$	$	$	$	$
Date							
1							
2							
3							
4							
5							
6							
7							
8							
9							
10							
11							
12							
13							
14							
15							
This month SUBTOTAL	$	$	$	$	$	$	$
16							
17							
18							
19							
20							
21							
22							
23							
24							
25							
26							
27							
28							
29							
30							
31							
This month ACTUAL	$	$	$	$	$	$	$
This month vs. PLAN	$	$	$	$	$	$	$
Year to Date PLAN	$	$	$	$	$	$	$
Year to Date ACTUAL	$	$	$	$	$	$	$
Year to Date ACTUAL vs. PLAN	$	$	$	$	$	$	$

SPENDING SUMMARY

This Month		Previous Month / Year to Date		Year to Date
Total Gross Income $_____		Total Gross Income $_____		Total Gross Income $_____
Minus Total Expenses $_____	**+**	Minus Total Expenses $_____	**=**	Minus Total Expenses $_____
Equals Surplus/Deficit $_____		Equals Surplus/Deficit $_____		Equals Surplus/Deficit $_____

>>> PurposeDriven®

MONTHLY EXPENSES

CROWN FINANCIAL MINISTRIES

Category	Transportation	Insurance	Household/ Personal	Medical/Family/ Professional	Entertainment/ Recreation	TOTAL EXPENSES	This Month SURPLUS/ DEFICIT
PLANNED AMOUNT	$	$	$	$	$	$	$
Date							
1						$	$
2						$	$
3						$	$
4						$	$
5						$	$
6						$	$
7						$	$
8						$	$
9						$	$
10						$	$
11						$	$
12						$	$
13						$	$
14						$	$
15						$	$
This month SUBTOTAL	$	$	$	$	$	$	$
16						$	$
17						$	$
18						$	$
19						$	$
20						$	$
21						$	$
22						$	$
23						$	$
24						$	$
25						$	$
26						$	$
27						$	$
28						$	$
29						$	$
30						$	$
31						$	$
This month ACTUAL	$	$	$	$	$	$	$
This month vs. PLAN	$	$	$	$	$	$	$
Year to Date PLAN	$	$	$	$	$	$	$
Year to Date ACTUAL	$	$	$	$	$	$	$
Year to Date ACTUAL vs. PLAN	$	$	$	$	$	$	$

MANAGING FINANCES GOD'S WAY – PRACTICAL APPLICATION WORKSHEET

PurposeDriven®

MONTHLY EXPENSES

CROWN FINANCIAL MINISTRIES

Month: _____ **Year:** _____

Category	GROSS INCOME	TITHE/GIVING	TAXES	Savings	Investments	Debt Repayment	Housing
PLANNED AMOUNT	$	$	$	$	$	$	$
Date							
1							
2							
3							
4							
5							
6							
7							
8							
9							
10							
11							
12							
13							
14							
15							
This month SUBTOTAL	$	$	$	$	$	$	$
16							
17							
18							
19							
20							
21							
22							
23							
24							
25							
26							
27							
28							
29							
30							
31							
This month ACTUAL	$	$	$	$	$	$	$
This month vs. PLAN	$	$	$	$	$	$	$
Year to Date PLAN	$	$	$	$	$	$	$
Year to Date ACTUAL	$	$	$	$	$	$	$
Year to Date ACTUAL vs. PLAN	$	$	$	$	$	$	$

SPENDING SUMMARY

This Month
Total Gross Income $_____
Minus Total Expenses $_____
Equals Surplus/Deficit $_____

+

Previous Month / Year to Date
Total Gross Income $_____
Minus Total Expenses $_____
Equals Surplus/Deficit $_____

=

Year to Date
Total Gross Income $_____
Minus Total Expenses $_____
Equals Surplus/Deficit $_____

PurposeDriven®

MONTHLY EXPENSES

CROWN FINANCIAL MINISTRIES

Category	Transportation	Insurance	Household/ Personal	Medical/Family/ Professional	Entertainment/ Recreation	TOTAL EXPENSES	This Month SURPLUS/ DEFICIT
PLANNED AMOUNT	$	$	$	$	$	$	$
Date							
1						$	$
2						$	$
3						$	$
4						$	$
5						$	$
6						$	$
7						$	$
8						$	$
9						$	$
10						$	$
11						$	$
12						$	$
13						$	$
14						$	$
15						$	$
This month SUBTOTAL	$	$	$	$	$	$	$
16						$	$
17						$	$
18						$	$
19						$	$
20						$	$
21						$	$
22						$	$
23						$	$
24						$	$
25						$	$
26						$	$
27						$	$
28						$	$
29						$	$
30						$	$
31						$	$
This month ACTUAL	$	$	$	$	$	$	$
This month vs. PLAN	$	$	$	$	$	$	$
Year to Date PLAN	$	$	$	$	$	$	$
Year to Date ACTUAL	$	$	$	$	$	$	$
Year to Date ACTUAL vs. PLAN	$	$	$	$	$	$	$

MANAGING FINANCES GOD'S WAY – PRACTICAL APPLICATION WORKSHEET

PurposeDriven®

MONTHLY EXPENSES

CROWN FINANCIAL MINISTRIES

Month: _____ **Year:** _____

Category	GROSS INCOME	TITHE/GIVING	TAXES	Savings	Investments	Debt Repayment	Housing
PLANNED AMOUNT	$	$	$	$	$	$	$
Date							
1							
2							
3							
4							
5							
6							
7							
8							
9							
10							
11							
12							
13							
14							
15							
This month SUBTOTAL	$	$	$	$	$	$	$
16							
17							
18							
19							
20							
21							
22							
23							
24							
25							
26							
27							
28							
29							
30							
31							
This month ACTUAL	$	$	$	$	$	$	$
This month vs. PLAN	$	$	$	$	$	$	$
Year to Date PLAN	$	$	$	$	$	$	$
Year to Date ACTUAL	$	$	$	$	$	$	$
Year to Date ACTUAL vs. PLAN	$	$	$	$	$	$	$

SPENDING SUMMARY

This Month		Previous Month / Year to Date		Year to Date
Total Gross Income $_____		Total Gross Income $_____		Total Gross Income $_____
Minus Total Expenses $_____	**+**	Minus Total Expenses $_____	**=**	Minus Total Expenses $_____
Equals Surplus/Deficit $_____		Equals Surplus/Deficit $_____		Equals Surplus/Deficit $_____

PurposeDriven®

MONTHLY EXPENSES

CROWN FINANCIAL MINISTRIES

Category	Transportation	Insurance	Household/ Personal	Medical/Family/ Professional	Entertainment/ Recreation	TOTAL EXPENSES	This Month SURPLUS/ DEFICIT
PLANNED AMOUNT	$	$	$	$	$	$	$
Date							
1						$	$
2						$	$
3						$	$
4						$	$
5						$	$
6						$	$
7						$	$
8						$	$
9						$	$
10						$	$
11						$	$
12						$	$
13						$	$
14						$	$
15						$	$
This month SUBTOTAL	$	$	$	$	$	$	$
16						$	$
17						$	$
18						$	$
19						$	$
20						$	$
21						$	$
22						$	$
23						$	$
24						$	$
25						$	$
26						$	$
27						$	$
28						$	$
29						$	$
30						$	$
31						$	$
This month ACTUAL	$	$	$	$	$	$	$
This month vs. PLAN	$	$	$	$	$	$	$
Year to Date PLAN	$	$	$	$	$	$	$
Year to Date ACTUAL	$	$	$	$	$	$	$
Year to Date ACTUAL vs. PLAN	$	$	$	$	$	$	$

PurposeDriven®

MONTHLY EXPENSES

CROWN FINANCIAL MINISTRIES

Month: [   ]   **Year:** [   ]

Category	GROSS INCOME	TITHE/GIVING	TAXES	Savings	Investments	Debt Repayment	Housing
PLANNED AMOUNT	$	$	$	$	$	$	$
Date							
1							
2							
3							
4							
5							
6							
7							
8							
9							
10							
11							
12							
13							
14							
15							
This month SUBTOTAL	$	$	$	$	$	$	$
16							
17							
18							
19							
20							
21							
22							
23							
24							
25							
26							
27							
28							
29							
30							
31							
This month ACTUAL	$	$	$	$	$	$	$
This month vs. PLAN	$	$	$	$	$	$	$
Year to Date PLAN	$	$	$	$	$	$	$
Year to Date ACTUAL	$	$	$	$	$	$	$
Year to Date ACTUAL vs. PLAN	$	$	$	$	$	$	$

SPENDING SUMMARY

This Month
Total Gross Income $_____
Minus Total Expenses $_____
Equals Surplus/Deficit $_____

+

Previous Month / Year to Date
Total Gross Income $_____
Minus Total Expenses $_____
Equals Surplus/Deficit $_____

=

Year to Date
Total Gross Income $_____
Minus Total Expenses $_____
Equals Surplus/Deficit $_____

PurposeDriven®

MONTHLY EXPENSES

CROWN FINANCIAL MINISTRIES

Category	Transportation	Insurance	Household/ Personal	Medical/Family/ Professional	Entertainment/ Recreation	TOTAL EXPENSES	This Month SURPLUS/ DEFICIT
PLANNED AMOUNT	$	$	$	$	$	$	$
Date							
1						$	$
2						$	$
3						$	$
4						$	$
5						$	$
6						$	$
7						$	$
8						$	$
9						$	$
10						$	$
11						$	$
12						$	$
13						$	$
14						$	$
15						$	$
This month SUBTOTAL	$	$	$	$	$	$	$
16						$	$
17						$	$
18						$	$
19						$	$
20						$	$
21						$	$
22						$	$
23						$	$
24						$	$
25						$	$
26						$	$
27						$	$
28						$	$
29						$	$
30						$	$
31						$	$
This month ACTUAL	$	$	$	$	$	$	$
This month vs. PLAN	$	$	$	$	$	$	$
Year to Date PLAN	$	$	$	$	$	$	$
Year to Date ACTUAL	$	$	$	$	$	$	$
Year to Date ACTUAL vs. PLAN	$	$	$	$	$	$	$

» PurposeDriven®

MONTHLY EXPENSES

CROWN FINANCIAL MINISTRIES

Month: _____   **Year:** _____

Category	GROSS INCOME	TITHE/GIVING	TAXES	Savings	Investments	Debt Repayment	Housing
PLANNED AMOUNT	$	$	$	$	$	$	$
Date							
1							
2							
3							
4							
5							
6							
7							
8							
9							
10							
11							
12							
13							
14							
15							
This month SUBTOTAL	$	$	$	$	$	$	$
16							
17							
18							
19							
20							
21							
22							
23							
24							
25							
26							
27							
28							
29							
30							
31							
This month ACTUAL	$	$	$	$	$	$	$
This month vs. PLAN	$	$	$	$	$	$	$
Year to Date PLAN	$	$	$	$	$	$	$
Year to Date ACTUAL	$	$	$	$	$	$	$
Year to Date ACTUAL vs. PLAN	$	$	$	$	$	$	$

SPENDING SUMMARY

This Month		Previous Month / Year to Date		Year to Date
Total Gross Income $_____		Total Gross Income $_____		Total Gross Income $_____
Minus Total Expenses $_____	+	Minus Total Expenses $_____	=	Minus Total Expenses $_____
Equals Surplus/Deficit $_____		Equals Surplus/Deficit $_____		Equals Surplus/Deficit $_____

PurposeDriven®

MONTHLY EXPENSES

CROWN FINANCIAL MINISTRIES

Category	Transportation	Insurance	Household/ Personal	Medical/Family/ Professional	Entertainment/ Recreation	TOTAL EXPENSES	This Month SURPLUS/ DEFICIT
PLANNED AMOUNT	$	$	$	$	$	$	$
Date							
1						$	$
2						$	$
3						$	$
4						$	$
5						$	$
6						$	$
7						$	$
8						$	$
9						$	$
10						$	$
11						$	$
12						$	$
13						$	$
14						$	$
15						$	$
This month SUBTOTAL	$	$	$	$	$	$	$
16						$	$
17						$	$
18						$	$
19						$	$
20						$	$
21						$	$
22						$	$
23						$	$
24						$	$
25						$	$
26						$	$
27						$	$
28						$	$
29						$	$
30						$	$
31						$	$
This month ACTUAL	$	$	$	$	$	$	$
This month vs. PLAN	$	$	$	$	$	$	$
Year to Date PLAN	$	$	$	$	$	$	$
Year to Date ACTUAL	$	$	$	$	$	$	$
Year to Date ACTUAL vs. PLAN	$	$	$	$	$	$	$

MANAGING FINANCES GOD'S WAY – PRACTICAL APPLICATION WORKSHEET

PurposeDriven®

MONTHLY EXPENSES

CROWN FINANCIAL MINISTRIES

Month: _____ **Year:** _____

Category	GROSS INCOME	TITHE/GIVING	TAXES	Savings	Investments	Debt Repayment	Housing
PLANNED AMOUNT	$	$	$	$	$	$	$
Date							
1							
2							
3							
4							
5							
6							
7							
8							
9							
10							
11							
12							
13							
14							
15							
This month SUBTOTAL	$	$	$	$	$	$	$
16							
17							
18							
19							
20							
21							
22							
23							
24							
25							
26							
27							
28							
29							
30							
31							
This month ACTUAL	$	$	$	$	$	$	$
This month vs. PLAN	$	$	$	$	$	$	$
Year to Date PLAN	$	$	$	$	$	$	$
Year to Date ACTUAL	$	$	$	$	$	$	$
Year to Date ACTUAL vs. PLAN	$	$	$	$	$	$	$

SPENDING SUMMARY

This Month		Previous Month / Year to Date		Year to Date
Total Gross Income $_____		Total Gross Income $_____		Total Gross Income $_____
Minus Total Expenses $_____	**+**	Minus Total Expenses $_____	**=**	Minus Total Expenses $_____
Equals Surplus/Deficit $_____		Equals Surplus/Deficit $_____		Equals Surplus/Deficit $_____

≫PurposeDriven®

MONTHLY EXPENSES

CROWN FINANCIAL MINISTRIES

Category	Transportation	Insurance	Household/ Personal	Medical/Family/ Professional	Entertainment/ Recreation	TOTAL EXPENSES	This Month SURPLUS/ DEFICIT
PLANNED AMOUNT	$	$	$	$	$	$	$
Date							
1						$	$
2						$	$
3						$	$
4						$	$
5						$	$
6						$	$
7						$	$
8						$	$
9						$	$
10						$	$
11						$	$
12						$	$
13						$	$
14						$	$
15						$	$
This month SUBTOTAL	$	$	$	$	$	$	$
16						$	$
17						$	$
18						$	$
19						$	$
20						$	$
21						$	$
22						$	$
23						$	$
24						$	$
25						$	$
26						$	$
27						$	$
28						$	$
29						$	$
30						$	$
31						$	$
This month ACTUAL	$	$	$	$	$	$	$
This month vs. PLAN	$	$	$	$	$	$	$
Year to Date PLAN	$	$	$	$	$	$	$
Year to Date ACTUAL	$	$	$	$	$	$	$
Year to Date ACTUAL vs. PLAN	$	$	$	$	$	$	$

))) PurposeDriven®

MONTHLY EXPENSES

CROWN FINANCIAL MINISTRIES

Month: _____ **Year:** _____

Category	GROSS INCOME	TITHE/GIVING	TAXES	Savings	Investments	Debt Repayment	Housing
PLANNED AMOUNT	$	$	$	$	$	$	$
Date							
1							
2							
3							
4							
5							
6							
7							
8							
9							
10							
11							
12							
13							
14							
15							
This month SUBTOTAL	$	$	$	$	$	$	$
16							
17							
18							
19							
20							
21							
22							
23							
24							
25							
26							
27							
28							
29							
30							
31							
This month ACTUAL	$	$	$	$	$	$	$
This month vs. PLAN	$	$	$	$	$	$	$
Year to Date PLAN	$	$	$	$	$	$	$
Year to Date ACTUAL	$	$	$	$	$	$	$
Year to Date ACTUAL vs. PLAN	$	$	$	$	$	$	$

SPENDING SUMMARY

This Month		Previous Month / Year to Date		Year to Date
Total Gross Income $_____		Total Gross Income $_____		Total Gross Income $_____
Minus Total Expenses $_____	+	Minus Total Expenses $_____	=	Minus Total Expenses $_____
Equals Surplus/Deficit $_____		Equals Surplus/Deficit $_____		Equals Surplus/Deficit $_____

PurposeDriven

MONTHLY EXPENSES

CROWN FINANCIAL MINISTRIES

Category	Transportation	Insurance	Household/ Personal	Medical/Family/ Professional	Entertainment/ Recreation	TOTAL EXPENSES	This Month SURPLUS/ DEFICIT
PLANNED AMOUNT	$	$	$	$	$	$	$
Date							
1						$	$
2						$	$
3						$	$
4						$	$
5						$	$
6						$	$
7						$	$
8						$	$
9						$	$
10						$	$
11						$	$
12						$	$
13						$	$
14						$	$
15						$	$
This month SUBTOTAL	$	$	$	$	$	$	$
16						$	$
17						$	$
18						$	$
19						$	$
20						$	$
21						$	$
22						$	$
23						$	$
24						$	$
25						$	$
26						$	$
27						$	$
28						$	$
29						$	$
30						$	$
31						$	$
This month ACTUAL	$	$	$	$	$	$	$
This month vs. PLAN	$	$	$	$	$	$	$
Year to Date PLAN	$	$	$	$	$	$	$
Year to Date ACTUAL	$	$	$	$	$	$	$
Year to Date ACTUAL vs. PLAN	$	$	$	$	$	$	$

))) PurposeDriven®

DEBT REPAYMENT SCHEDULE

CROWN FINANCIAL MINISTRIES

CREDITOR:		**Date:**	
Describe What Was Purchased:			
Amount Owed:		**Interest Rate:**	
Total Number of Payments:		**Monthly Payment:**	

Payment Number	Amount Paid	Payments Remaining	Balance Due
1	$		$
2	$		$
3	$		$
4	$		$
5	$		$
6	$		$
7	$		$
8	$		$
9	$		$
10	$		$
11	$		$
12	$		$
13	$		$
14	$		$
15	$		$
16	$		$
17	$		$
18	$		$
19	$		$
20	$		$
21	$		$
22	$		$
23	$		$
24	$		$
25	$		$
26	$		$
27	$		$
28	$		$
29	$		$
30	$		$
31	$		$
32	$		$
33	$		$
34	$		$
35	$		$
36	$		$
37	$		$
38	$		$
39	$		$
40	$		$
41	$		$
42	$		$
43	$		$
44	$		$
45	$		$

PurposeDriven®

DEBT REPAYMENT SCHEDULE

CROWN FINANCIAL MINISTRIES

CREDITOR: _____ **Date:** _____

Describe What Was Purchased: _____

Amount Owed: _____ **Interest Rate:** _____

Total Number of Payments: _____ **Monthly Payment:** _____

Payment Number	Amount Paid	Payments Remaining	Balance Due
46	$		$
47	$		$
48	$		$
49	$		$
50	$		$
51	$		$
52	$		$
53	$		$
54	$		$
55	$		$
56	$		$
57	$		$
58	$		$
59	$		$
60	$		$
61	$		$
62	$		$
63	$		$
64	$		$
65	$		$
66	$		$
67	$		$
68	$		$
69	$		$
70	$		$
71	$		$
72	$		$
73	$		$
74	$		$
75	$		$
76	$		$
77	$		$
78	$		$
79	$		$
80	$		$
81	$		$
82	$		$
83	$		$
84	$		$
85	$		$
86	$		$
87	$		$
88	$		$
89	$		$
90	$		$

PurposeDriven®

DEBT REPAYMENT SCHEDULE

CROWN FINANCIAL MINISTRIES

CREDITOR: _____ **Date:** _____

Describe What Was Purchased: _____

Amount Owed: _____ **Interest Rate:** _____

Total Number of Payments: _____ **Monthly Payment:** _____

Payment Number	Amount Paid	Payments Remaining	Balance Due
1	$		$
2	$		$
3	$		$
4	$		$
5	$		$
6	$		$
7	$		$
8	$		$
9	$		$
10	$		$
11	$		$
12	$		$
13	$		$
14	$		$
15	$		$
16	$		$
17	$		$
18	$		$
19	$		$
20	$		$
21	$		$
22	$		$
23	$		$
24	$		$
25	$		$
26	$		$
27	$		$
28	$		$
29	$		$
30	$		$
31	$		$
32	$		$
33	$		$
34	$		$
35	$		$
36	$		$
37	$		$
38	$		$
39	$		$
40	$		$
41	$		$
42	$		$
43	$		$
44	$		$
45	$		$

))PurposeDriven®

DEBT REPAYMENT SCHEDULE

CROWN FINANCIAL MINISTRIES

CREDITOR: _____   **Date:** _____

Describe What Was Purchased: _____

Amount Owed: _____   **Interest Rate:** _____

Total Number of Payments: _____   **Monthly Payment:** _____

Payment Number	Amount Paid	Payments Remaining	Balance Due
46	$		$
47	$		$
48	$		$
49	$		$
50	$		$
51	$		$
52	$		$
53	$		$
54	$		$
55	$		$
56	$		$
57	$		$
58	$		$
59	$		$
60	$		$
61	$		$
62	$		$
63	$		$
64	$		$
65	$		$
66	$		$
67	$		$
68	$		$
69	$		$
70	$		$
71	$		$
72	$		$
73	$		$
74	$		$
75	$		$
76	$		$
77	$		$
78	$		$
79	$		$
80	$		$
81	$		$
82	$		$
83	$		$
84	$		$
85	$		$
86	$		$
87	$		$
88	$		$
89	$		$
90	$		$

PurposeDriven®

DEBT REPAYMENT SCHEDULE

CROWN FINANCIAL MINISTRIES

CREDITOR: _____ **Date:** _____

Describe What Was Purchased: _____

Amount Owed: _____ **Interest Rate:** _____

Total Number of Payments: _____ **Monthly Payment:** _____

Payment Number	Amount Paid	Payments Remaining	Balance Due
1	$		$
2	$		$
3	$		$
4	$		$
5	$		$
6	$		$
7	$		$
8	$		$
9	$		$
10	$		$
11	$		$
12	$		$
13	$		$
14	$		$
15	$		$
16	$		$
17	$		$
18	$		$
19	$		$
20	$		$
21	$		$
22	$		$
23	$		$
24	$		$
25	$		$
26	$		$
27	$		$
28	$		$
29	$		$
30	$		$
31	$		$
32	$		$
33	$		$
34	$		$
35	$		$
36	$		$
37	$		$
38	$		$
39	$		$
40	$		$
41	$		$
42	$		$
43	$		$
44	$		$
45	$		$

PurposeDriven®

DEBT REPAYMENT SCHEDULE

CROWN FINANCIAL MINISTRIES

CREDITOR: _____ **Date:** _____

Describe What Was Purchased: _____

Amount Owed: _____ **Interest Rate:** _____

Total Number of Payments: _____ **Monthly Payment:** _____

Payment Number	Amount Paid	Payments Remaining	Balance Due
46	$		$
47	$		$
48	$		$
49	$		$
50	$		$
51	$		$
52	$		$
53	$		$
54	$		$
55	$		$
56	$		$
57	$		$
58	$		$
59	$		$
60	$		$
61	$		$
62	$		$
63	$		$
64	$		$
65	$		$
66	$		$
67	$		$
68	$		$
69	$		$
70	$		$
71	$		$
72	$		$
73	$		$
74	$		$
75	$		$
76	$		$
77	$		$
78	$		$
79	$		$
80	$		$
81	$		$
82	$		$
83	$		$
84	$		$
85	$		$
86	$		$
87	$		$
88	$		$
89	$		$
90	$		$

Life Insurance Worksheet

This sheet is designed to give you an approximation of your life insurance needs. It is not intended to be precise, and it does not take into account the effects of inflation. Seek the counsel of a professional advisor to determine your needs more accurately.

Once you have determined how much life insurance you need, compare that to the amount you currently have. Then, if needed, analyze your spending plan to determine how much new insurance you can afford. Seek experienced counsel to decide the precise amount and type of insurance that would meet your needs and budget.

- **Present annual income needs:** How much money is currently required to meet your family's needs?

- **Subtract deceased person's needs:** How much of that income is currently being spent to meet the needs of the person who is being insured? For example, the costs associated with their car, clothing, food, medical bills, etc., that you will no longer have to pay.

- **Subtract other income available:** What is the total amount of additional income sources, such as survivor's salary, social security benefits, and retirement accounts?

- **Net annual income needed:** This is the amount of income that will need to be supplied each year through insurance benefits.

- **Insurance required to provide needed income:** This is the amount of the insurance death benefit required to meet your net annual income needs.

- **Lump sum needs:** Include any debts or large expenses you would like to pay off in the event of death.

- **Debts:** What is the total amount of debt you want to pay off?

- **Education:** How much would you like to provide for your children's education?

- **Total Life Insurance Needs:** Add the insurance required for income and lump sum needs. This is an estimate of the total amount of life insurance you should have.

MANAGING FINANCES GOD'S WAY – PRACTICAL APPLICATION WORKSHEET

PurposeDriven

LIFE INSURANCE WORKSHEET

CROWN FINANCIAL MINISTRIES

Name: John and Jane Sample

Date: January 1

GROSS MONTHLY INCOME	
Present annual income needs:	$ 73,200.00
Subtract deceased person's needs:	$ 6,000.00
Subtract other income available: (Social Security, Investments, Retirement)	$ 40,000.00
= Net annual income needed:	$ 27,200.00

Insurance required to provide needed income: Net annual income needed, multiplied by 14.29 (assumes a 7% after-tax investment return on insurance proceeds)	$ 388,688.00

Lump sum needs:

Debts:	$ 20,375.00
Education:	$ 40,000.00
Other:	$ -
Total lump sum needs:	$ 60,375.00

TOTAL LIFE INSURANCE NEEDS:	$ 449,063.00

PurposeDriven®

LIFE INSURANCE WORKSHEET

CROWN FINANCIAL MINISTRIES

Name:

Date:

GROSS MONTHLY INCOME	
Present annual income needs:	$
Subtract deceased person's needs:	$
Subtract other income available: (Social Security, Investments, Retirement)	$
= Net annual income needed:	$

Insurance required to provide needed income:

Net annual income needed, multiplied by 14.29 (assumes a 7% after-tax investment return on insurance proceeds)

$

Lump sum needs:

Debts:	$
Education:	$
Other:	$

Total lump sum needs: $

TOTAL LIFE INSURANCE NEEDS: $

Introducing the new small group edition of 40 Days of Purpose

Based on the best-selling book, *The Purpose Driven Life* by Rick Warren, this new curriculum is uniquely designed for church members and new believers who desire to fulfill God's purpose for their lives.

The 40 Days of Purpose Small Group Edition is also great for those who want to review the material in their new or existing small group/class, share it with a friend, or even for pastors who want to review the five purposes with their church family in the new year.

Inside Out Living — "Blessed are the poor in spirit, for theirs is the kingdom of heaven."
With there words, Jesus introduces a whole new way of living—inside out living! The "Sermon on the Mount" is a blueprint for building the Christian life. From the book of Matthew this series shares Jesus' teachings on worry, forgiveness, integrity, loving our enemies, storing up treasures in heaven, and many other topics.

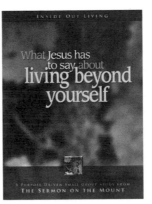

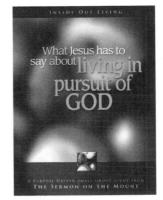

What Jesus has to Say about Living a Blessed Life

What Jesus has to Say about Living Beyond Yourself

What Jesus has to Say about Living in Pursuit of God

Purpose Driven® Life Small Group Series is designed to lead a small

group through one chapter of *The Purpose Driven Life* each week with a fifteen minute video lesson taught by Rick Warren. This small group study helps your group learn each of the five purposes through a time of reflection and application.

Vol. 1: What on Earth Am I Here For?
Vol. 2: You Were Planned for God's Pleasure
Vol. 3: You Were Formed for God's Family
Vol. 4: You Were Created to Become Like Christ
Vol. 5: You Were Shaped for Serving God
Vol. 6: You Were Made for a Mission

A Spiritual Road Map in a Mixed up World — 1 Thessalonians is

packed with relevant and important teaching for you, your small group and your church. This wonderful letter is important not only for its significance as the Apostle Paul's first letter, but also because of the guidance it offers us today for living the Christian life.

Volume 1 topics address spiritual growth, discipleship, pure motives, spiritual reproduction, and love for people.

Volume 2 topics address sexual purity, loving insiders and reaching outsiders, spiritual laziness, small group living, and preparing for the return of Jesus Christ.

Vol. 1: Six Lessons from 1 Thessalonians 1:1–3:13
Vol. 2: Six Lessons from 1 Thessalonians 4:1–5:24

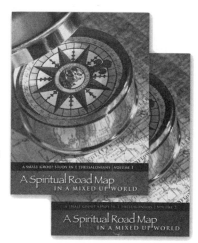

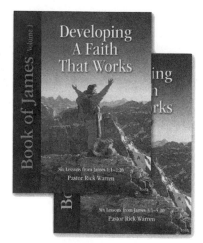

Developing a Faith That Works — Engage your

small groups in an enriching verse-by-verse study of the book of James. Each of the two volumes contain video curriculum with six lessons taught by Pastor Rick Warren. An accompanying study guide has lesson outlines with fill-ins to complete during the teaching and discussion questions.

Vol. 1: Six Lessons from James 1:1–2:26
Vol. 2: Six Lessons from James 3:1–5:20

The Purpose Driven® Life Journal — Allow the Scripture to speak to you. Use this beautiful leather-bound journal to record your reflections, questions, and insights from daily readings of *The Purpose Driven Life*.

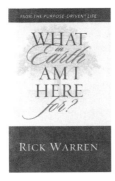

What on Earth Am I Here For? Mini Booklet — Impact every person who enters your church by offering the insights of *The Purpose Driven® Life* compacted into a mini booklet. This booklet features the first chapters of *The Purpose Driven® Life*, updated for purpose-seeking people.

The Purpose Driven® Life for Commuters

A new abridged audio CD for commuters—listen while you drive to work, ride the bus, or take the subway. Rick Warren will guide you through a personal 40-day spiritual journey.

COMING SOON!
LIFE GROUP E-NEWSLETTER

GET THE LATEST NEWS IN SMALL GROUP MINISTRIES AND TOOLS, INSIGHTS AND TECHNIQUES TO HELP YOU GROW A HEALTHY SMALL GROUP MINISTRY. WE'LL ALSO KEEP YOU UP-TO-DATE ON WHAT'S NEW IN SMALL GROUP STUDIES AND MORE! SIGN UP TODAY AT: WWW.PASTORS.COM/LIFEGROUPNEWS

Crown Money Map™ — With over 100,000 units distributed in its first printing, the *Crown Money Map*™ is a visual guide to true financial freedom that shows 7 Destinations to becoming financially free. This step-by-step, full-color trip of a lifetime has a fun and simple layout, and you will be encouraged as you take each step along this important journey.

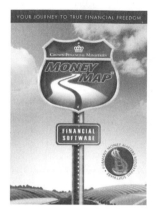

Crown Money Map™ Financial Software
— *Crown Money Map*™ *Financial Software* is a PC-bsed budgeting solution and is designed to help ease your financial burdens by doing a lot of the thinking for you. It keeps track of dates, budgets, and other details. Print checks, make deposits, track your portfolio. And biblical advice is always only one click away! Many new features make this software easier to use.

Crown™ Mvelopes® Personal — *Crown™ Mvelopes® Personal* is a Web-based budgeting option that allows you to manage your spending online—anytime, anywhere! It tracks your spending, and you always know how much is left to spend in every budget category. Get started with a free 30-day trial—visit Crown.Mvelopes.com for details.

Business By the Book Independent Study

Learn How To:

- Integrate principles from Scripture with your daily practices
- Grow your company profitably
- Develop leadership skills and grow in Christ so that you will be more like him as a business leader

Practical Counsel On:

- Hiring and firing decisions
- Pay increases and promotions
- Guidelines for selecting managers
- Employee pay decision
- Borrowing and lending decisions
- Forming corporations and partnerships

Free and Clear — Almost half of all American families spend more than they earn. Along with the obvious financial challenges, skyrocketing debt leads to increased stress, compromised health and devastated relationships. God has a better way!

The ABC's of Handling Money
God's Way — This world teaches kids that money and possessions are a source of self-worth. Nothing could be further from the truth. *The ABC's of Handling Money God's Way* is an excellent tool to combat these fallacies and teach children basic principles of working, giving, saving, and spending. This colorful, story-based workbook will engage children and keep them interested as they learn that God's plan for handling our finances is so much better than the world's way. Recommended for ages 5–7.

The Secret of Handling Money God's
Way — Four children with a financial challenge learn the secret of giving, saving, spending, and much more. They also discover that they can trust God to provide. The principles are embedded in an exciting story of adventure that captures and holds the attention of children. This colorful, story-based workbook will engage children as they learn that God's plan for handling our finances is so much better than the world's way. Recommended for ages 8–12.

The ABC Learning Bank — *The ABC Learning Bank* has been designed to
teach your child the value of money and how to handle it in a way that is pleasing to God. It is a fun, 3-compartment bank made of transparent plastic. Each of the 3-compartments (giving, saving, and spending) can easily be separated—no more taking your entire bank with you! New stopper design is more durable and user-friendly. Free parent's pamphlet and audio CD is also included when you order from Crown.

The Genius of Generosity — What's so genius about generosity? After all, our world celebrates people who have learned how to have it all . . . not those who have learned to give it all away! If you'd like to learn principles for wise giving and generous living, this audio series by Chip Ingram will both challenge and encourage you. Learn the genius of generosity and expand your portfolio of eternal rewards!

Walk Thru the Bible partners with local churches around the world to take God's Word to the world in relevant ways for lasting life change through high quality resources and seminars.

TO ORDER PRODUCT OR FOR MORE INFORMATION:
WWW.WALKTHRU.ORG OR CALL 1.800.763.5433

CHRISTIAN FINANCIAL PROFESSIONAL NETWORK

One of the greatest unrecognized and unmet needs in the body of Christ today is the ability to find a financial professional who shares a biblical perspective on stewardship. Christian Financial Professionals Network is here to meet the need, offering both personal and professional financial resources, and referrals to a network of certified financial professionals who are equipped to integrate biblical counsel with financial counsel.

CFPN exists to minister to Christian financial professionals and teach them how to incorporate biblical principles into the services they offer clients. Through three, 2-1/2 day training sessions, professionals can attain CFPN Certification™ in the following disciplines:

- Financial Planner (Comprehensive Planning)
- Accountant (Personal Income Tax, Corporate Income Tax)
- Investment Advisor (Fee-only Investment Management)

- Investment Consultant (Commission-based Investment Management)
- Insurance (Insurance Agent)
- Lawyer (Estate, Wills, Trusts, Planned Giving, etc.)

Additional membership benefits include:

- In Focus CD Magazine
- Members-only web connection
- Quarterly newsletter
- CFPN e-news update
- Discounts on resources and certification training

Christian Financial
Professionals Network
There is a difference

For more information about CFPN Certification and requirements, or CFPN resources, visit www.CFPN.org